## Quotes and Testimonials

"This book makes it easy to see how design and advertising can work effectively for your Company too, no matter what its size."
**Clive Williams, Commercial Manager, Vitax Limited**

"Having taken a good look at this book I thought how VERY useful it would have been when I started – and I'm in the design business! As a sounding board and guide to taking a different perspective on how to present and promote a company, Sid Gibson's experience enables anyone to make more informed decisions."
**Roger Fuller, International Design Consultant**

"Even as a small enterprise the ideas in *Does My Firm Look Big In This?* worked very well for us and helped to build the reputation we enjoy today. It's so important to get those essential first steps right."
**Gary Rivers, Partner, Branscombe House**

"The secret is getting your logo right at the start, and then everything follows on from there. This book shows you how."
**Max Williams, Managing Director, Climax Windows Limited**

"Every executive should have a copy for reference, refreshment and reflection. It is easy to read and I would have found it of great assistance in the past."
**Warwick Bergen, Director, The Triangle Partnership Limited**

For a complete list of Management Books 2000 titles
visit our web-site on http://www.mb2000.com

# DOES MY FIRM LOOK BIG IN THIS?

*Top tips to help make the most of how small businesses are perceived*

**Sid Gibson**

2000

First published in 2008 by Management Books 2000 Ltd
Forge House, Limes Road
Kemble, Cirencester
Gloucestershire, GL7 6AD, UK
Tel: 0044 (0) 1285 771441
Fax: 0044 (0) 1285 771055
Email: info@mb2000.com
Web: www.mb2000.com

British Library Cataloguing in Publication Data is available

ISBN 97818525859

Printed and Bound by Digital Book Print Ltd

# Acknowledgements

I would like to thank the many friends and colleagues who supported the idea behind *Does my Firm look big in this?* David and Julie Yule for enthusiastic encouragement to get on and write the book. Time Heap of Logomotion (www.logomotion.co.uk) for invaluable help on the technicalities of web site building. Angela Podmore of Kinetic Public Relations (www.kineticpr.co.uk) for guidance on the professional way to tackle PR. Peter Hadley of Squarefox Design (www.squarefox.co.uk) for development and origination of my cover design. Finally my wife Jane for her patience with my fits of pique when the words would not come right, and for endless cups of coffee.

# About the Author

Sid Gibson is a Design Consultant advising on corporate identity, advertising and related promotional activities. Clients are offered the benefits of impartial planning, creative concepts, and copy-writing together with project management of design development, origination and production with third party resources. He is a Fellow of The Chartered Society of Designers, and in 1972 was elected Member of The Institute of Practitioners in Advertising. Following appointment as Creative Director with a long established Birmingham advertising agency and subsequently becoming Managing Director, he started his own advertising agency. This ran successfully for eleven years before being sold to a large Group. Experience of working 'on the client side' of advertising and marketing, was gained as Head of Design, Oppenheimer UK, London, and as Design and Corporate Identity co-ordinator, Fortes Foods Group, London and Birmingham. He was an exhibitor at 'Ten Midlands Designers' sponsored by the Chartered Society of Designers in Birmingham, and his packaging design work has been exhibited in Design Council, London. Diverse consultancy experience with many clients includes:

Amari Metals
Argos retail Group
Cadbury Schweppes
Delta Metals
Development Board for Rural Wales
Energy Services Division of Midlands Electricity Board
Fortes Foods Group
Glynwed International
Hitachi UK and Europe, together with their distributors
Hydrovane UK
Hymatic Aerospace division of FR Group
Kubota UK
Midlands Electricity Board
Shell UK
Vitax Chemicals

# Contents

# Read this right now

There!

I bet you wouldn't have bothered to read a 'Preface' or 'Prologue' or 'Foreword' or 'Introduction'. Sounds boring, so you'd best cut to the chase and get on with reading the top tips – that's what you've got this book for, isn't it?

But hold on a moment. Let's be quite clear on this before you start. *Does My Firm Look Big In This?* is not a heavyweight textbook with definitive answers on every technical aspect of promotion, advertising and corporate identity for the smaller company. It is a guide to the general principles involved, and to the practical approaches you can adopt to make sure you find the right solutions for *your* company, to create the right impression to generate business – and above all, to ensure that your company is perceived at least on a par with its much bigger competitors.

In the course of reading this book, I hope that you will learn something important, and *useful*, about making design and advertising work for your firm, some pitfalls to watch out for, and be much better equipped to talk to professionals on equal terms. It's how you *approach and manage* these issues which is important.

There are many ways to build your corporate identity, and make your firm look the way you want it to look. However, the problem is that there are just as many (if not more) ways to damage or dilute your corporate identity, and make your firm look nothing like the way you want it to look. There are right ways and wrong ways to approach these issues. This book will help you to distinguish between the two. And remember always that more important than how *you* want your company to look, is how *your customers* expect it to look when they're about to spend money on what you want to sell to them.

As you will see, what you look like in visual terms is just part of the story; but this is where you must start, and because of that, it's where I shall begin. Later on we'll have a look at how these essential visual beginnings form the bedrock for a successful corporate identity, and then we'll appraise the fundamentals of implementing perceptions of identity through some of the never-ending manifestations of advertising and promotion which your firm may need to consider.

So, every one of these top tips is designed to help you to find the 'right' ways to achieve success whether that's in corporate identity, brand image, product packaging, services branding, advertising, public relations, direct mailing, SMS, promotions, exhibitions, media presence, point of sale, literature, printing, website building, marketing... See what I mean? No one can tell you how to do it all but when it's down to you to make it all happen – and not many small businesses enjoy the luxury of employing full-time specialists who enable you get on with your proper job – here's some information you can use for making clued-up decisions on how to *approach and manage* these issues. The good news is that every one of these 'right' ways works for organisations across the whole gamut of commerce and industry – and they'll work for your firm, too.

As a simple example, 'Read this right now' probably made you more likely to read on than 'Preface' or 'Prologue' or 'Introduction', because it sounded more interesting and stimulated a response. It gives the impression of being a bit different, and sets the scene for what's to come rather better. And making the most of how your firm is perceived means setting the scene to create a more effective environment for selling. That's what this book is all about.

Which brings us to the first tip.

---

*Tip*

**Making sure your firm looks good makes it more engaging and easier for customers to choose you over the competition.**

---

# 1

# It's no big deal!

So why is it so important to make the most of how your firm is perceived? In the real world, does it really matter what you look like? Isn't spending money on image an unnecessary expense you could well do without? Surely image is just fluff and totally disengaged with the substance of business?

According to Government statistics there are over 2.1 million VAT/PAYE registered businesses in the UK alone. In 2005 (the most recently available statistics at the time of writing, and I don't expect the figures change much year on year) there were over 177,900 new registrations for VAT. Imagine, everybody fighting to get their new born company recognised and noticed – that's some challenge! Let's also remember all those outfits which don't operate VAT along with individuals earning their living who may also be competitors in your field.

Here's another thought for you. I suggest that there are many people out there who would be interested in what you have to sell – but they don't know who you are. They don't know what your firm does, they don't recognise it, what its name stands for, or where it's located. And in today's competitive environment with so many alternative sources of supply, they probably don't care that much, either. Until you tell them.

Are these reasons enough to convince you why it's important to make the most of how your firm is perceived at every opportunity? There are more.

Consider visual image and the way in which you use words to describe your company both as an introduction to new buyers (after all, first impressions count) and as a reassurance for established ones. Use visuals and words skilfully and you'll have powerful sales tools as important as any other in your armoury.

When you've created the right kind of identity, your business will be promoted and recognised wherever it goes resulting in benefits you'll find a lot more tangible than simply cobbling things together as you go along according to any odd short term requirement of the moment.

Who looks at your firm, anyway? Or who might be looking at it tomorrow? It may be easy to think some people won't matter or would never wield any influence on your plans, but developments often take companies in unforeseen directions. Diversification, take-over, merger, and succession, for example. Think about how you would like your firm to look and be regarded in five years' time. What will its reputation be then? What sort of reputation would you like it to have? Will your identity truly represent what this is? Such questions will help to focus decisions about the people you should be targeting right now.

It starts with you, of course. You need to be happy with the firm's image – and no one else is likely to be looking at the firm's identity more closely – a point worth remembering if you find yourself becoming too busy and distracted (and introverted) to keep an eye on the broad picture. Then there's staff and possible future employees; your customers; your potential customers; your suppliers; public bodies such as local authorities (you might need planning permissions later on); banks and other business influences such as chambers of commerce; local organisations, clubs and societies with customers as members; newspapers, magazines and other media on the look out for stories and news.

The short answer then to who looks at your firm is 'lots'. Lots of impressions. Lots of influences. Lots of opinions.

Despite this seemingly alarming disparity of onlookers, you don't have to spend loads of money creating the right kind of identity to meet their expectations– whatever your firm's size. In practice, it has been my experience that clients actually save money by thinking in advance and properly controlling their identity across everything they do.

Control, that's the secret.

What do I mean by 'properly' controlling identity? When you've got products or offering services that are selling okay, why worry? Let it all hang out (you might think) and just carry on regardless of what you look like. Get it sold. Move on.

Conversely when you're small or just starting out and not much is being sold there are more vital things to worry about than your identity. Surely finance, or distribution, or manufacturing – even finding customers – are infinitely more important?

Well, tell that to M&S, BMW, Shell, or Virgin – or any of the successful big names in business who you might consider could take liberties with their image since they are selling on such a huge scale. Is it a surprise to learn they take enormous care to ensure total consistency of identity and style? I bet you'll not find it too difficult to recall what they look like. There are demanding rules which everyone is supposed to follow, although even here it's not hard to spot deficiencies which can lead to a call for re-branding. Fashion and the desire to keep up to date have also been known play their parts too.

What works for big names will work for a small business too, no matter whether it's a start-up in growth mode or already established and in need of a makeover. By the same token, ask a market trader selling fruit and vegetables whether it's worth the trouble of setting up a great-looking display. You'll know the answer to that already.

There is little doubt that the effective use of good design and a consistent style of words and language for presentation of sales messages create a positive identity and are vital components in achieving and maintaining long-term business success. Evidence of the combined effectiveness of visuals and words surround us every day both in the high street and at home from retail shopping centres to packaging, catalogues and brochures, TV, magazine and newspaper advertising.

Successful names – and successful people – do it properly because an integrated, easily recognisable, well presented and apt identity provides tangible, proven sales benefits way beyond just 'looking nice'.

Despite the benefits there is still too little understanding, or indeed too much misunderstanding of the importance of design. This is brilliant news for you, because you can exploit this knowledge to gain an advantage over competitors, maximise opportunities to promote your firm's strengths and uniqueness, and be confident of immediate recognition – and because you'll have a visibly firm base upon which to build, the route for introducing new products or services will be made smoother, and probably a lot cheaper.

'But a just a moment,' I hear someone saying. 'These principles are all very well, but what about when you're just starting up and there is literally no money in the pot for this kind of thing?'

I would answer this by suggesting that whatever the financial constraints you will be spending money on essential basic elements, such as printing letterheads or signage to use from day one, so you may as well do it right. Conversely, if you really haven't the cash to start properly, are you sure you shouldn't wait until you have? Please remember that every principle on identity expressed here remains relevant whatever its breadth, depth, style, or scale of implementation. And after all, there's no benefit whatsoever in not thinking in advance – there are huge benefits to properly controlling your identity *from the start*, however tiny the budget might be.

It's no big deal. It's simplicity in itself. The benefits are real, proven, and worthwhile. Just do it right from the start!

> *Tip*
>
> **Think in advance and stay in control.**

# 2

# Identity

There is a lot of confusion about 'corporate identity', and what it actually means in practice. A surprising number of people think it is a purely visual concept. However, there is a distinct difference between 'identity' and 'visual image' – though it is to the latter that most organisations attribute their own perceptions of 'identity'.

Wrong!

It is a proven fact that people perceive your business on many levels, and not just by seeing its 'visual image', key as that is. There's the name, for a start. Can it be easily pronounced or is its meaning misinterpreted on occasion? What about feel and touch of the stationery you use or the packaging you send out? Does your office or reception area smell fragrant? Do letters leaving the firm always get typed and signed off in the same style? What do you think the customers' experience of dealing with you is like? How do they react? What will they say to others about your van driver or the person who answered the telephone? Did they like the attitude of the individual who took their order or the salesperson in the showroom? Is that perception of the firm consistent across all your business and social contacts and not just clients or customers? What about employees, suppliers, competitors, the media, local authorities and so on? We're back to that long list again. And it's not only of people looking at you – but a wide variety of people forming opinions about who you are and what you stand for from many other angles, all different to that of a visual impression.

The dividing line between visual and non-visual perceptions of your company is in practice always going to be somewhat blurred. Is the image being lived up to or is it failing to do justice to the services you give, for example? You can begin to understand why those strict rules of consistency are fundamental keys to success.

Like it or not, yours and every business under the sun has an identity, and a reputation which may be something different from what's intended. There is obviously no benefit in being vague about how you want be seen (as an organisation which people want to work with, work for, or buy from), so it is vitally important to make the most of how your firm is perceived at every opportunity you can think of. It is in your power to control that identity and manage how your business appears to the world on every level.

To complicate the issue even more, we have 'brand image', where corporate identity and visual image converge together on your products and packaging – but that's another story, not to mention your press and public relations profile! More of these later.

Before moving onto these subjects let us first take a look at what you need to consider from a design perspective. Later we'll have a look at useful pointers for successful implementation of those design elements across wider aspects bearing in mind that any differences between 'visual image' and 'corporate identity' should be acknowledged and are inextricably linked. To make a success of them both, always look for the big picture, take a calculated overall view, and remember to stay in control of what is happening to your identity and image.

Because things can change without you noticing!

---

*Tip*

**Remember your business is always judged at every level, so stay in control.**

---

# 3

# A beginning

So where do you start in all this?

First by knowing what you really want from an identity. Then promise yourself you will stick with it, live its values and clearly communicate that message come what may. Commit to setting an example for all to see; encourage colleagues and staff to understand the firm's identity and live its values; aim to recruit those who will be comfortable adopting those philosophies.

Knowing what you really want from an identity might sound obvious but as I have already said, many businesspeople, perhaps because they dismiss design as being beyond the balance sheet and not clearly quantifiable as a profit creator, simply do not recognise the long term benefits within their grasp. In many instances these benefits have come as a revelation to clients of mine who adopted a policy of planning a corporate identity within the framework of a coherent sales and marketing programme.

It is important to be *decisive* about the sort of company you would like to be known as – consider it as a projection of corporate 'personality' in ways that ultimately influence people to buy. Knowing what you really want will not only be of enormous help when you get round to briefing your professional advisors, but will also minimise costs and keep the reins on future planning by keeping stuff 'tied down' to a coherent plan. The inevitable clutter of accumulated essentials from printed bill heads to vehicle livery is destined to erode for ever your precious identity if you don't watch out. Things have a habit of attaching themselves unnoticed as time passes. It follows from this that everyone in the organisation must also know where you're coming from and be on your side fighting for its values. It is vitally important to make absolutely certain you are getting continued support throughout the company if ultimate results are to be achieved, especially as you grow.

Before we start, have you a name for the firm yet? If so, you may like to skip the next few paragraphs because I'm going to tell you a story. It's a true one but for obvious reasons which you'll understand, I've manipulated the name and industry to save causing embarrassment.

I was called in by a long established family firm of removers to overhaul their identity because of an intended change of name due to their expanded international services. They had been known for many years as Sidney Haulier Transport and Sons Co Ltd, the name writ big across the side of the wagons.

My brief included instructions to create a logo using the initial letters of the proposed new name of 'Sidney Haulier International Transport'.

I looked across the boardroom table and asked if that was what they really wanted. My question was greeted by blank stares. In the clamour of becoming 'international' in stature, everyone had missed seeing the big picture.

I leave you to draw your own conclusions on whether the job went ahead on that basis!

The moral of the story, if you are at the point of deciding on a name for the firm, is to look at the ramifications of how it will look, and indeed how it sounds. Speak it out loud. Speak it softly. Get others to say it. Does it sound like your firm already? Is it easy to pronounce and spell? What does it look like written down? What does it look like typed in capital letters and in lower case letters? Can it be misinterpreted? Does it reflect the kind of business you're in? Is it appropriate? Will it stand the test of time?

It's always wise to find a name which is likely to stand the test of time whatever the field of operation. If it sounds even slightly quaint and out of date, or conversely too fashionable and all the rage right now, what will it say about your business in ten years time? For example 'Ace Audio Cassette Repairs' probably wouldn't work well today and certainly not very much further into the future. 'Ace Audio' on the other hand might. Keep it plain, simple, easy to use, and long lived.

Remember, any name, whether it's you're own or an invented one, always looks different when in print. As soon as that name appears in a design it becomes part of a wider network of communication and has direct connotations with what you are trying to sell. It is part of the company image whatever its typeface and colour turn out to be, however and wherever it's used. Consider these facts before you make a final decision because hopefully, you'll be living with it for a long time.

Incidentally, the technique of saying names out loud and listening to someone else also works well with advertisement headlines and the like. Try it using any headline in the press and you'll see.

So, name resolved, is your company to look traditional? Modern? Like a bank? Like a department store? Similar to an international manufacturer? A local one? Use your favourite colours? Appear low-cost, or expensive? High tech? Fun? Deadly serious? The permutations are endless, but only you can decide – in fact must decide, if others both in the firm and working as your design advisors are to be clear and confident about what they are trying to help you achieve. Ask yourself what 'tone of voice' do you associate with your business and its brand, or its services – loud, subtle, dynamic, patient, understanding, street-wise, cultured and so on. The choice is endless and you might even have a little *fun* deciding what works best. Then, when you've decided, you'll have to interpret that in visual terms, and keep in mind the need for it to be reflected at all times in your printed promotional messages however and wherever they appear. We're back to seeing the big picture and staying in control again.

You might argue that as you're paying a designer in the first place, isn't it their job to decide how the firm should be interpreted in visual terms? Well yes, but if you are able to point them in the direction of your thoughts on the subject it will give them a head start thus saving them time, and you money.

As you can see, that decision of knowing what you really want is very important. There have been times when my clients said they didn't know what they wanted and asked for guidance. When ideas and visuals were ultimately presented they suddenly knew what they didn't want, but said the ideas helped them to decide what they did!

This is an expensive way to go, a designers dream of an open cheque book job if you're feeling cynical, so make up your mind, and decide what you really want as early as you can.

---

*Tip*

**Know what you really want – and stick with it. Then
ensure everyone else involved knows too.**

---

# 4

# The difference between
# good and bad design

We have a problem here to know what exactly is good – or bad – design.

When it comes to visual appearance, everyone has a different opinion on what looks good – or bad. Look at the wallpaper in the house next door to yours! Sure, you could say your letterhead looks neat, or the van livery sticks out a mile on the street, but neatness or 'impact' do not necessarily constitute good design for an identity. We'll have to use that consistency word again, but even consistency of implementation is only one of a number of the 'non-visual' elements of good design you can use to help yourself arrive at a right decision. After all, part of the dictionary definition states that design is 'for a plan, purpose, or intention', and artistic opinion of whether it is good or bad doesn't really come into it.

The difference between good and bad design is not the difference between what looks good and what doesn't look good (always a subjective judgement), but the difference between a design that achieves the desired objective (in terms of visual impact) and one that does not.

Take a look at the local farmers leaflet illustrated on page 22; it was stuffed into my weekly delivery of organic vegetables. Is this good design? When measured against the sophistication of international companies many would say it looks horrendous, but that opinion would miss the point. On this evidence one is tempted to conjure up an argument which says there is no such thing as bad design at all, because if Five Penny Farm had used a slick full colour leaflet to promote organic beef their particular appeal of 'back to basics in a very small way' brand would be lost. The inference here of 'basic' is in itself a promise of quality. It is an identity just as clearly understood for what it means as any highly sophisticated one. So this is good design. You know exactly what to expect. Am I confusing you yet?

*Farm leaflet*

The limitation of course with this illustration is that, as an identity, it is going nowhere. As a one-off leaflet it says what it means, but it would be a challenge to adopt such a style in a meaningful way across a business which has plans for expansion and promote a range products in, say, the way Wiltshire Farm Foods have done so successfully (see page 23). There is still a similar offer of good food delivered to your door, but on a sophisticated scale needing far more resources to fulfil the assurances of a large scale advertising program backed by an efficient sales distribution network. The presentation of

Wiltshire Farm Foods reflects convincingly both the high quality of product and the standards of service which customers can expect.

*Wiltshire Farm Foods leaflet*

As we have seen, good design it more than just good aesthetics. Design solutions have to be relevant, practical to live with, and reflect contemporary style. It can help here to look closely at some of the big names in business and see how they tackle the problem. Take a fresh look – indeed a fresh look from a standpoint you may not have considered in the past – to see how they manage their typography in conjunction with photography on an advertisement for example. See how these techniques and styles can be recognised in the ads of other companies. Much of what you determine will be down to contemporary style – fashion if you like – and it is important to take these factors into account to keep your visual appeal 'up there'. Then you may find it equally illuminating to take a more calculating look at the image portrayed by smaller commercial enterprises and see how often they get it wrong.

Apart from the foregoing exercise on style and fashion, when mulling over designs for your identity make sure 'non-visual' aspects are taken in to account on whatever ideas come up.

Will these ideas be capable of being developed and translated and reproduced in many different forms and sizes without giving printing (especially newspaper printing) problems? Do they rely solely on colours to be recognised? (They shouldn't!) Will they be legible and recognisable in one colour? Can they be integrated successfully in product branding or packaging? Do they use any non-standard difficult-to-obtain 'exclusive' typefaces? (They shouldn't!) Can they be fitted onto a multitude of (possibly yet unknown) items because they have been designed with flexibility in mind? Do designs conflict with the identity of any competitor's? (It's not difficult to end up looking very similar when fulfilling similar briefs in the same line of business, so check everyone out carefully – you don't want problems of copyright and intellectual property rights rearing their ugly head.) Do they promote an 'overall' style and feel to the identity? (You should not be dependent on just a logo for recognition.)

And finally, which of the designs set your heart racing when you imagine them being used to promote your business?

When all's said and done, it will be down to you (again) to see the difference between good and bad design, and you'll have to choose one of those 'right' ways more likely to make your firm look the way you want it to look rather than one of the wrong'uns. Just keep the 'non-visual' considerations in mind and you'll find it easier to come to a decision.

> *Tip*
>
> **Remember that good design is not just visual.**

# 5

# Your visual image – another subjective issue?

This is quite a short chapter but a vital one. It will take less time to read than carrying out the actions I suggest, but I think you'll find it very worthwhile.

Do you know what your firm looks like? Does it look good, bad, or indifferent? How does it stack up against those strict consistency rules? What do other people think about the way you look? It's sometimes hard to know, particularly when, as we saw in the previous chapter, opinions on what constitutes 'good' design varies so much.

Here's something you can do which goes some way to answering these questions.

First find a blank wall. Then assemble images or examples of all – and I mean *all* – the visual items used in day-to-day running of the business. Take every item of stationery; ferret out every insignificant piece of printed paper you use; cut out any ads you may have run (not forgetting classifieds and directory entries); photograph the outside of your building and every vehicle on the fleet; sort out all the promotional material produced in the past two years.

Then stick everything together on your blank wall. That's what you look like.

Looks good does it? Or can you see room for improvement? And do you wish there was some way to avoid the expense you're about to incur on a rehash?

By the way, on a non-design related front do you need every item you see? This may be an opportunity for you save a bit of money by reducing or combining the functions of some of the stationery. Control your identity in all of its manifestations and you'll have both practical and financial pay-backs as well.

However, let's get back to visual considerations of design.

Look more closely and I'll wager you'll find inconsistencies. Typesetting that doesn't quite match up – line spaces and font changes for example, layout and content of address details (you'd be surprised how frequently this one pops up), variations of colour and quality of paper-stock, vehicle livery sullied by lettering which breaks clumsily across panel joints. And so on. Be ruthless in your evaluation. Even the smallest inconsistencies you find do matter because, as I've already said, such details are destined to erode for ever your precious identity if you don't watch out.

What you might find exasperating, if ground rules have never been established, is the fact that you won't know when items are wrong or indeed what they're supposed to look like in the first place!

Before you rush in and make changes, or dismiss the exercise as a waste of time because you've discovered you look brilliant, don't forget to ask your customers for their opinion. While you're at it ask the staff, and your suppliers too, even down to the helpful van driver who innocently delivers that expensive stationery which doesn't hang together.

Now for those dear readers who may not have reached this far in their new company's development, I can tell you from past familiarity with such problems that the foregoing exercise will undoubtedly reveal weaknesses you can avoid if you follow the tips in this book! The moral again is – start right and know what you really want, then save money by thinking in advance and properly controlling your identity and every activity associated with it.

---

*Tip*

**Make time to take care of the details that keep your firm looking good.**

---

# 6

# Get a logo – or not

Logos, symbols, badges, crests, icons, emblems, motifs – call them what you will – are usually considered to be an intrinsic part of how you look. All you need do is get a decent logo designed, slap it on everything and your firm's identity is half way done, then?

No! No! No! No! No!

The most basic rule of building a successful identity is broken – or forgotten – in even the biggest businesses you can think of by indiscriminate application of 'the logo'. It's my opinion that this is because employees down the line responsible for buying supplies and services such as printing or placing advertisements often simply do not know or understand the importance of where the boss is coming from or what the firm's policy on identity is supposed to be. (Please read 'A beginning' again.) The investment made in establishing your ground rules to create a personality for the business is wasted if all your time and trouble results in just a logo being stuck on to things. It's like a clown's mask being worn – could be anybody!

Of course it's the usual thing for a company to want to use a logo (or symbol, badge, crest, emblem, motif) as part of their identity, but before you embark on the process of getting one designed, begin with the premise that in isolation neither your name nor your logo will mean anything to anybody. However, the very design of the logo can suggest something about your company even before it becomes associated with what you're selling, and that's why it is important to make that suggestion work positively for you right from the start.

Let me explain.

Just for fun we'll create a new company name which reverses the word 'logo'. OGOL.

Means nothing to you? Thought not!

Now what might the name 'OGOL' mean to you if you saw it out of context but written in a particular style of lettering? What type of business might that company be in? Imagine the name in a classic kind of Roman and it might be a staid financial concern. In chunky lettering with a fat shadow it may be a fast food outlet. Then again a bargain basement household goods store may well use a brash, racy sort of brush script. Whilst each of these styles would carry a different 'tone of voice' they do not convey 'personality'. In fact, without some unique visual feature, typography on its own seldom works convincingly as a logo which is likely to enlighten anyone what the business is all about, let alone lend it a personality.

There is an inevitable vagueness about what a name exposed in this way means, and typographical logos will inevitably need substantial support from an identity programme to have any hope of effectiveness. (Don't imagine these as 'designed' logos by the way, just the name in simple typefaces, or even hand-written in different ways to illustrate the point. Such a basic solution to creating a logo obviously needs to be enhanced, exaggerated, stretched, distorted, reversed out of solid shapes, colours added and so on. Then it might work. Hey, we're designing already!)

But supposing 'OGOL' represented, for example, 'Original Garden Objects Limited' and some poor soul somewhere is struggling to run a business on the assumption you will understand what he's trying to sell. We know now that 'OGOL' means nothing as a name and needs propping up somehow.

So perhaps none of those basic configurations of letters are appropriate after all, but what say if we added an underlining graphic of grass, or a border representing carved stone? Immediately there's a degree of relevance introduced that connects the logo with the company's activities, even though the name in itself still means nothing.

The moral here is that you should always look for relevance in your logo design (or symbol, badge, crest, emblem, motif) and make sure it works hard to connect with what you do. Just as important, if not more so, is to consider the framework in which it will be used. Make it fit in with the whole style of your identity programme, your grand plan if you like, and view the surrounding areas of your logo as part of it. Many companies establish a border, or a fixed space around the logo upon which other elements are never allowed to encroach, but if you build your identity properly with inbuilt rules for consistent implementation from the start, this should not be necessary as a separate rule – but you can make it one if you like.

*An illustrated logo*

For the record, whilst 'logo' is the term accepted by all and used in everyday business language to mean an emblem or graphic device used to identify an organisation, let's be clear on its definition as compared to symbols, badges, crests, emblems or many other possible descriptions of identity insignia with ideas stretching back through history on national and regimental flags, heraldry and so on.

There is often confusion on the issue, but a logo, short for logotype, is always a graphic design concoction or arrangement of the actual letters or initials of the firm's name. The term logotype in actuality means a slug of metal type used by printers and comprises a word or group of letters. A symbol can be an abstract shape, or an illustration of some kind either representing what you do or be purely decorative like an animal or bird, as some High Street banks for instance. Badges and crests of course are self explanatory, but exploiting a coat of arms might be viewed as old fashioned or literally a sham. Obviously you can use combinations of these definitions and indeed putting logos and symbols together is common practice evident the world over. The trick is to make sure people know the logo belongs to you, that it can be read and understood, and that it bestows a distinctive personality upon your business.

It doesn't matter what your preference is as long as you remember consistency of implementation is paramount for success. While on the subject of consistency, never, ever let your logo (symbol, badge, crest, emblem) be 'bastardised' by inappropriate use such as upside down, printed in the 'wrong' colours or treated to special effects. It is the face of your firm – don't let it be disfigured. (After the face, the rest of the firm's body is its corporate identity by the way.)

Consistency doesn't mean everything has to boringly identical. Think of family members in uniforms of different ranks and you'll get my drift. Consistent and recognisable, each with their own character but not identical.

On the other hand, you may not choose to have a logo (or symbol, badge, crest, emblem) and simply use your firm's name or your own, in an appropriate typeface, or font design. At least this will be cheaper than paying for design and artwork. I say appropriate typeface because the font style has to reflect your kind of business and not chosen just because you seen it elsewhere on something else and liked it.

So it's fine to use just your name, but as we've observed earlier, in isolation it will mean absolutely nothing to anybody and unless you are BP or equally well known, it will be sensible to state what the firm does as an integral part of the name. Ensure the font you pick is readily available and not too 'off the wall' and it will make implementation easier when you use different suppliers.

Let me briefly digress here and touch on the terminology used for typefaces, or fonts as they are more generally known. I have experienced surprisingly robust discussions on the choice of typeface, down I suspect to a combination of personal preferences coupled with a frankly staggering array of styles. Many of these might look very similar but have different names because they come from different producers. This can be confusing especially as new ones are coming out all the time.

However to keep it simple, typefaces can be broadly divided into four groups and you can refer to them as such: Roman which has serifs, Sans Serif which are plain characters, Scripts and Decorative styles.

From these basics there are literally thousands of variations: Blocked serif (called Egyptian), expanded Roman, condensed sans, light sans, copperplate, calligraphic, shadowed Roman, shadowed sans, stencil style, outlined everything, and so on. The list goes on indefinitely with opportunities to select typefaces giving very distinctive effects and which reflect exactly the essential qualities you need for your firm. You must insist that your designer shows you typeface catalogues and the wide range of alternatives available to you.

If you do decide to attach a 'what the firm does' or a 'strap line' alongside the name, and this also applies to the logo or symbol, badge, crest, emblem if you employ a strap line, use it all the time so that it continues to reinforce recognition and consistent messages about the firm.

The downside to adopting this course of action is that you surrender a significant element of individuality which may make the company name less memorable because other people will be able to use the same font for their name too. And at the end of the day it's not the best use of your hard-earned to promote visibility for another company competitor or not, whilst at the same time taking the risk of creating confusion for your customers about who you are.

Whatever route you take, remember to look for possible problems in reproduction on the many and varied applications the logo will have to face through its life. Newsprint for example is notorious for clogging up an image due largely to the softness of the paper and the speed at which papers are printed. You may have to consider special versions of the logo to meet such restrictions and for this reason it is prudent to avoid logos with fine line work detail and shadows constructed with delicate tints. A tint can be reproduced by using a 'half tone screen' of the base colour. (A 'half tone screen' is made up of a fine grid which creates tiny dots virtually invisible to the naked eye. This is how all printing is done, both in full colour and black and white. Look through a magnifying glass at a photograph in a newspaper and you will be able to spot its limitations and see how a half tone works in principal).

You'll also have to make certain that it reproduces successfully in all sizes from miniscule print on stationery or packaging through to the expansive dimensions required for signage and exhibition stands. A few years ago I remember being impressed with a mailing booklet from a Dutch printing firm which was launching a new identity. The cover of the book was simply divided into two bright colours (red and yellow) which turned out to be a magnified close-up section of their new logo. Pages two and three were covered in a pattern of tiny logos all perfectly reproduced in many different colours. Images on subsequent pages zoomed out to show the logo in different forms and applications such as stationery and vehicles. This zooming out concept continued to the last page spreads which revealed the logo painted across the roof of their building and, as a final flourish, a field next to it mown in the logo shape.

The point here was that not only had the new logo and corporate identity been shown to be working exceptionally well in visual terms, but also the quality of printing and booklet production had served as an excellent demonstration of the company's abilities. The whole exercise had relevance to both the message and the kind of business they operated.

I believe that this example is an admirable principal to remember. Your corporate identity will work best when viewed as a coherent whole being. It isn't just a logo. Think about the graphic applications on all the things the business uses as an extension of the intrinsic style and visual values of the logo. The whole corporate identity, all of its component parts must in effect be the logo for the firm.

I began this chapter by contesting the notion that 'All you need do is get a decent logo designed, slap it on everything and your firm's identity is half way done then?' Now that we've examined various options and considerations for the creation of your logo we shall see how to make it work, and work well for you across every facet of your business.

The dominant thing to remember – and I make no apologies for banging on about it again – is to be passionate about consistency of implementation. This might sound simple and straightforward but inconsistencies are the downfall of many otherwise successful identity programs.

## Registering your logo

I'm going to digress slightly here for a bit, and touch upon a subject not part of the creative process and which can be put into place at any time, but possibly best done sooner rather than later. It's something which bothers some more than others – a lot depends on your aspirations and the competitive (or not) environment in which you operate.

Having finally decided on your logo (or symbol, badge, crest, emblem), is it worth registering the design as a trademark to stop others copying it?

Well, yes and no. I have to be ambiguous here but the fact is that there is no legal requirement to register your mark because your design is automatically protected by common law. Basic copyright protection also comes into play and you must ensure that copyright is assigned to you by your designers when they are paid so that you can use your logo as and when you wish. There will be a little more information on this later on.

The issue is potentially somewhat complex and may need your serious consideration beyond the compass of this text. However, in broad principal should you *not* register your design, another party can register a similar design, or even the same design and stop you using yours, unless you can prove plagiarism. Similarly, if you *do* register, it makes it easier to stop another party from using a design similar to yours. In other words, whilst registration cannot stop others using your logo it will discourage them and make them more aware of possible legal action if they do copy it. You will have statutory monopoly to use your logo and can choose to stop others using it on the same or even similar services and goods. Conversely, a registered trade mark can help build confidence and trust when giving your permission for independent agents or franchisees *et al* use your design.

Another often overlooked reason for registering a logo is that it gives the opportunity to search and make sure there is not another one out there already. Most small businesses launch out and hope for the best. After all, registration costs money and you will have to decide whether this is worthwhile taking into account the expense of any defence proceedings in the future. You may also feel that if you have already registered as a limited company, the name itself suffices to identify your company as a unique entity.

You can go through the process of registering through the UK Patent Office but it is advisable to consult a solicitor and ask to be pointed in the direction of a trademark or patent agent specialising in this work, especially if you require registration in countries other than UK.

Incidentally, there is often confusion about the difference between copyright and trademarks. Put simplistically, copyright protects literary, artistic, and musical works – i.e. what you write about yourself in literature and ads, and the graphics used to present and sell your firm, along with your promotional jingle if so minded. Trademarks essentially distinguish the goods and services offered by different companies, and by definition also incorporate an element of copyright. See?

Where there are little 'TM' or '®' or '©' marks included with a logo (or symbol, badge, crest, emblem). 'TM' simply informs that it is considered a 'trademark' and may or may not have been registered. '®' means it has been registered. '©' simply identifies that the originator of a work is confirming ownership. That's why you may see '©' on the presentation material of your designer's initial ideas! It doesn't in practice give any additional protection beyond that afforded by common law.

It is also worth clarifying who really owns the copyright of your logo. When you pay a designer, or a design company for work produced as part of your brief, copyright will normally belong to you or your company. No problems there then.

If, however, the designer you've briefed subcontracts and hires a freelance artist or designer, for example to produce a specialist illustration or even a photograph, then that aspect will belong to him because he is commissioning that work and paying the bill not you – or even worse, to the artist, if the position is contractually clear . The answer to this little conundrum is to ensure all copyrights are assigned to you at the outset.

---

*Tip*

**Don't ever, ever mess with the logo once it's established, and make sure it consistently endorses your identity across everything.**

---

# 7

# Any colour you like as long as it's...?

What's your favourite colour? Have you always fancied a chunky pink or piercing shade of brown as the colour to mark out the unique qualities of your firm? Colour is/was/always will be the most subjective part of your decision making in the creation of your visual image. Almost certainly!

You see, engineers unremittingly like dark blue for their letterheads whilst hairdressers will always prefer a lighter, peacocky sort of shade. And it is just this kind of stereotyped thinking which gives you the chance to be different and separate your firm from the competition.

Subjectivity in colour choice is further compounded by a compulsion to ask others 'do you like this, or this one best?' – the answer to which prompts uncertainty about your decision, not to mention the obvious problems with people who are colour blind and cannot tell the difference anyway!

The only rule you need to remember about colour is that there really isn't a hard and fast one. However, colour does unquestionably help define identity and complements the 'tone of voice' set by both your logo design and the messages of your promotional material. So with such an important constituent it's essential to be vigilant in considering your options however subjective they turn out to be. The priorities are to make sure you're using colour to differentiate your products or services and to make that colour is relevant to what customers expect to see.

Some say the best colours for corporate use are red and blue. Certainly a firm favourite is blue and its hues, and you can see these everywhere. Blue means dependable, and is cool. Red conveys energy and a feeling for getting things done.

Black might be viewed as exclusive and sophisticated – but nevertheless has to be the undisputed workhorse of text to say the least! Not only that, but have you ever seen a website in black and white? Not so sophisticated after all perhaps, but there again so much depends on how it's used.

Green is associated with environmental friendliness, nature, and balance. If you'd like to appear safe or pure use plenty of white space, while grey will promote an aura of neutrality.

Is your business in a vibrant, youthful market? Think about mixing bright primary colours together.

The topic of colour psychology has far-reaching ramifications and my commentary here is but a trigger for your thinking on the subject. Just try to avoid a brief insisting that your designer uses your favourite colour – because it just might not work best for you with commercial success foremost in your mind.

Having said that, however, my clients usually have colour preferences, and with the caveat that it needs to be appropriate to the business, I would go as far as to say any colour can be successfully accommodated by an accomplished designer. Combinations of dissimilar colours are a different thing altogether and I have been (and let me be diplomatic here) *surprised* at some requests made on occasion!

Don't make it hard for people to see, though. Not everyone has perfect vision – delicate pale yellow on a white background might mistakenly be considered a good choice for a florist, but if the name is difficult to read, who's going to bother trying?

On a more pragmatic note, don't dismiss any colour until you've seen a sample used in a comparable format to the one you intend (brochure, letterhead, etc). This is obviously part of the design process and should be carefully evaluated at both the designer's colour visual and the printer's proof stages. Don't get it printed and live in hope! What might look great (or ghastly) as a swatch can be transformed when integrated across the various shapes and nuances of your identity programme.

It is crucial to make sure your basic corporate colours are available as standard printer's inks – i.e. not special mixes as this will cause endless matching problems in the future. Ensure it is also obtainable in standard paints and vinyl colours for signs, vehicles, buildings, and exhibitions. Undoubtedly there will be need at some time (newspaper advertisements or those local charity programmes you support for example) for your logo to appear in one colour – usually black.

Printers and designers generally use 'PMS' colour references, an internationally recognised printing, packaging and publishing system providing an accurate method for specifying and matching colour reproduction. PMS (Pantone Matching System) originated in USA but is pretty much used universally these days. The thing to watch out for, however, is that because of uncontrollable fading of pigments and paper ageing, you should ensure the PMS colour swatch being referenced for your identity programme is up to date – no more than two years old, I reckon. These colour swatch books tend to hang around a lot longer than this and if open and exposed to light for long periods, quite significant variations can occur. PMS colour swatches are always dated so it is easy to check.

It's also crucial to keep in mind that printed inks vary enormously on different materials. You'll note the differences especially on matt and gloss papers. Avoid arguments and at all times insist on seeing proofs on the correct material! Your designer's initial presentation should give a fairly good representation of the finished result but even here it's possible to get the wrong impression, so discuss the issue thoroughly.

---

*Tip*

**Be careful before committing colour schemes. Be certain you understand how colours reproduce on the finished materials.**

---

# 8

# Do you actually need a professional designer?

So, we've arrived at the point of knowing what you really want, have an insight into the principles of creating a name, a logo, setting up a colour scheme and looking forward to making the most of how your business is perceived. What's next?

You could think of having a go and generate some designs on your computer if you have the time! Or getting that young lad next door who's such a whiz on the internet to print out a few ideas. You know what to look out for, after all. Computers these days are such brilliant assets for any business, so let's get them to work and really see what they can do. It's relatively easy to manipulate a few fonts and end up with a half decent job, hand it over to a printer on a disc which can be modified to suit his printing method and the paper he has in stock. Not only that, but you could also buy that software programme allowing you to build your own website and organise mail order sales at the same time. Job done then?

You can always tell jobs produced by amateurs. More significantly, you can always tell jobs produced by professionals. Perhaps I should qualify that by saying true professionals. Unfortunately I have to tell you that not everyone engaged in matters of design and promotion is necessarily 'professional' in either the standard of creative work or indeed the quality of service they provide. It is to be hoped that you will be able to have a positive opinion on aesthetic standards of work when looking at examples of a designer's earlier assignments, but quality of service can be another issue altogether. This is a lot more difficult to evaluate.

If you can, before commissioning anyone, contact some of the designer's clients and ask a few questions. Did the designer understand and grasp the brief with enthusiasm? Were those clients happy with the ideas presented? Was the job delivered on time? Was it within budget? Did a printer have any technical difficulties with origination supplied? You'll generally find people happy to share their experiences of creative work and they'll wax lyrical about the really good ones delivered hand in hand with a professional attitude. That makes your decision easier. In any event it should not take long before a clear picture emerges.

It's thankfully unusual, but I have known of incidents in the past where some unscrupulous character has attempted to pass off the design work of others as their own. It seems to happen particularly when someone's 'gone freelance' after working for a bigger group. Claiming to have 'worked on a project' is a variation on this theme but is not the same as being responsible for it. Find out exactly what their involvement was. As I say, such situations are relatively unusual but obviously undesirable and something you should be aware of.

The other side of the coin is the brazenly successful designer or design group, who seem to maximise opportunities to impress you. This leads to an element of suspicion that should you become a client you are going to be ripped off – did you see all those new motors in the car park? You may even get the impression that they don't really regard their work as a proper job because half of them look like a bunch of nattily dressed arty-farty oddballs. In truth they can be a bunch of serious people too, whose job it is to 'identify, design, advertise, and promote', and as such their apparent flamboyance with flash cars, stylishly furnished premises, and fashionable clothes is perhaps understandable. You'll discover their success is rarely down to ripping off clients with inferior work. More like they have rich clients who simply demand top class work.

Then again, brilliant designers with impeccable business credentials can appear positively scruffy!

This combination of disparate abilities and allegedly suspect ethical standards makes the selection process difficult to say the least, and adding complication to the conundrum, creative work is in itself notoriously subjective too. Here is what you must do. Initially, it's going to take up quite a chunk of your valuable time. I can assure you, however, it will be time well spent and you will find it both enjoyable and informative.

You have doubtless gathered that I do not condone a DIY job. Unless you are in the business, there is no way you can keep up with fast moving developments in materials, the preparation of optimum quality origination, or computer and web-building technology, not to mention tricky details such as search engine optimisation and legislation for printed literature and advertisements. You will also have to spend a fortune on software and the training to know how to use it. Neither will you have the benefit of cross fertilisation of design and copy writing ideas that come through working with a broad array of clients in many different, multi-faceted industries. As I said, you can always tell jobs produced by amateurs, can't you?

It may be hard to find a shortlist of designers to whom you would like to talk because surprisingly not many advertise themselves or are publicised outside trade publications. As mentioned earlier, you could contact a company whose promotional material you have noticed and ask for their designer's name. To start from scratch to find local sources there are always telephone and business directories, but it may prove a little tedious to plough through a long list of names you've never heard of.

You may like to begin your search with the Chartered Society of Designers (CSD) which is the world's largest chartered body of professional designers and governed by Royal Charter. As such its members are obliged to practice to the highest professional standards, so if a designer has MCSD or FCSD after their name you can be assured of a professional service.

You can learn more about CSD at www.csd.org.uk. Other informative sources are www.newdesignpartners.com and www.designcouncil.org.uk.

It's really best to have a personal recommendation by someone either in the business of design, media or advertising, or who has had experience of working with an individual designer as a client. If this is not possible and if you don't already know a designer, a design studio or an advertising agency who you feel happy with, here are some additional options to consider.

# Printers

Some printers – not all of them – can offer a basic design service of reasonable quality but by definition they do so because they want your printing business. Some of my printer friends may disagree but I say they are primarily in business to print, and in that context design work has to be considered an add-on. Sometimes they offer this add-on work for free. Furthermore, keeping original design ideas, production and printing with one restrictive source is not going to be best for the variety of applications your identity programme will need in the long term. Keep your options open.

In any event, unless you specifically pay for the design work, remember copyright remains the property of the firm you appoint and if you wish to swap printers for any reason there could be problems. You can make it a condition of appointment that copyright in all design work they do for you is assigned to your ownership, either automatically or for a separate fee. Unless you own the copyright you will not be able to reproduce your 'own' designs in different media without consent. Just because you have paid for say printing a leaflet, does not automatically mean you can take or adapt that design for use elsewhere. (Incidentally, the printer is also entitled to destroy his film and plates after printing – you do not own *them*.) In small-scale work, copyright issues do not usually become major problems but the law is highly complex. Be aware of your position and if in doubt seek legal advice.

I am convinced that the most effective route to securing a successful visual image for implementation across a broad field over a long time is by employing the services of a professional designer. How do you know which one is right for you? Someone working independently? In a 'group' which is sometimes referred to as a 'design agency' or 'design consultancy'? If you have big plans for promotion on a wider scale a designer working in an advertising agency will have the support of a lot more besides design. In this case you'll be appointing the agency for its overall in-house skills and wide ranging resources, not just for it's design team.

Let me explain the differences, although confusingly they frequently call themselves different things so please allow a little leeway. In principle though, you'll find the following a reasonable guide. I hope!

# Independent designers

A designer working independently – or 'freelance' or 'design consultant' – can often provide superb standards of creativity. Often but not always. You will have to take a good look at their portfolio of work and make up your own mind. These people survive alone in the harsh world of commerce because they are very good at what they do and can even be highly sought-after for ideas by other design groups and advertising agencies as well as other clients like yourself. The disadvantages can mean a lack of financial resource, for example to buy print competitively on your behalf, and you may find yourself tearing your hair out because you are unable to contact them simply because they are on holiday or off on another important job somewhere else. Ask what computer system they have. The industry standard format is Apple Mac and if by any chance they are using a standard PC to prepare origination for printing, or ads for newspapers and magazines, be wary. Having said that, if you are planning to manipulate or adapt their designs for other applications, and you work on a PC system, it obviously makes sense to have the design produced in a PC-formatted file. From the printing perspective there is no difference in the quality of output from Apple Mac or PC systems.

Professional qualifications are obvious indicators of ethical principles (see CSD), but in my experience there are also many excellent designers who have no formal qualifications but who have 'been through the mill' of industry to build their expertise and experience. Creativity and professionalism are not exclusive preserves of formally qualified 'art school trained' designers. As I say, take a good look at their portfolio and form your own opinion.

## Design groups, design agencies, and design consultancies

The number of designers employed and their collective ability, not to mention areas of specialisation or range of services, can vary considerably. From the top down, beware the likely costs from leading name consultancies that beautifully wrap up everything in-house from basic graphics and print-buying to media-planning and sophisticated full-colour double-page-spread magazine advertisements, with packaging design and point-of-sale production thrown in. You may also find on the menu such things as direct mail distribution, poster site scheduling, exhibition stand and interior design, product design and public relations. Yes, there are fabulous design groups around who provide a comprehensive facility verging – or merging – with that of a full service advertising agency and more besides, but they are expensive to hire and more often than not based in London or major city centres.

If it's not a leading name consultancy able to turn down work offering limited financial return, one of the problems which may face a largish group of, say, ten designers is keeping everybody busy all the time. This is why you might find an enthusiastic willingness to have a go at anything! However, as we have already observed you can't do everything yourself – at least not to the high standards upon which you will insist, and that applies to designers too. In such circumstances it is best to ask what their policy is on subcontracting work to freelancers. This is standard practice in the business, particularly to specialists providing things such as illustration, technical drawing, photography, copywriting, website design and so on. Because of professional pride not all design companies want to admit to this and hide such activities beneath the cloak of 'trade secret'. I oppose such policies. I believe it builds a stronger working relationship if you know what's going on and are encouraged to meet any third party involved to ensure you stay in control and that your brief is properly communicated and fully understood.

That said, creative types are by nature insecure and you would not of course wish to undermine their confidence by mistrusting their ability to communicate your brief to a third party. Would you?

If you do find some of your work has been subcontracted to an individual make certain that copyright issues are taken care of at the outset. It is the freelance designer who automatically retains intellectual property, if the group from whom you are buying has not made sure (contractually) that they are acquiring copyright. Even if the group does have copyright, this may be limited to the primary use of the freelancer's work. Check it out.

You will not I think, experience quite the same reticence to offer transparency of working practices in smaller design groups of three or four. They accept more readily the need for outside help on occasion and are not afraid to admit it. In fact, I think this can strengthen considerably the case for choosing a smaller group – their costs are likely to be lower, you do not necessarily have to compromise on breadth or expertise of individual services and your business will become a more significant factor within their turnover figures – not to mention showing off your work in their portfolio which I can assure you is a prized and valuable tool for them to help win more clients such as yourself!

There is another category of small design groups which deserves your consideration and that is of newly qualified art and design college leavers who get together to make a name for themselves. Standards of creativity can be very good (and prices cheap or ambitious depending on what their lecturers have told them) but experience of business practice can be patchy leading to possible problems on technicalities at production stage. Again, check out their working methods, facilities, and computer systems, etc. You'll also have to become more involved in getting the job completed through printing or implementing media schedules as well as ensuring legal issues are met (for example size of text on packaging or claims made in ads or direct mailshots).

Take time to look at the work of as many designers as you can. Visit them; have a good look around the studio; chat to staff if possible and get to know if you're likely to be able to build a happy and dynamic working relationship with them. Not only will this help you to put individual quality standards into perspective, but you will also gain an insight into their business and learn to talk knowledgeably on equal terms, not least of which is understanding what some of the buzzwords and jargon mean!

## Website designers

A website designer is a different animal to your graphic designer for print. Fact!

You will undoubtedly come across those who claim to do both equally well but in practice the two disciplines are very different. This is not to say website designers do not have to be skilled in graphics or that your designer for print is unable to produce something for you to see on your website, but to be totally effective, web design needs the addition of specialised wide-ranging technical knowledge and experience. Without these you simply won't get maximum return for your money and whilst you can buy cheap web design using standard templates, your saving will turn out to be a false economy in the long term. And note that with standard templates and software you may have problems successfully integrating your visual identity and end up looking suspiciously like your competitor, or many others on the internet for that matter who may have used the same template.

To check that your designer knows what he is talking about, and that he knows what will work on the web to give you the results you need, here are some questions to ask.

## How will positioning my website within search engines be accomplished?

A knowledgeable web developer will know that a search engine optimised (SEO) website is in fact a human optimised site. 'Content is King' is the mantra of SEO experts. The search engines' algorithms are designed to deliver relevant content, so your websites copy must be well written and informative and the site should also be designed for user-friendly access to both sighted and disabled people. The search engines use a browser technology very similar to text readers used by blind people. After content relevance, the next most important factor affecting your site's position in the search engines is how many websites link to your pages. Getting reciprocal links (I'll link to you if you link to me) is OK, but a one-way link from an established site, with a good ranking, could be more potent than dozens of reciprocal links from friends. Beware anyone who says they can guarantee a top ten position; they are probably using 'black hat' techniques and could get your site blacklisted.

## Will you be using any 'black hat' SEO techniques?

Underhand Search Engine Optimisation techniques include hidden text, for example white text on a white background, this increases the number of key words visible to the search engines without visitors seeing the duplication. Other techniques include keyword stuffing which basically means repeating words an unnatural number of times.

## What design elements are going to help the shopper / enquirer find the answers they are looking for?

Good site navigation is vital and it should be expandable as the site grows. The navigation menus should be intuitively organised. If your site is large, a good search facility that delivers accurate results will be expected by your visitors.

## Who will own my domain name?

You must own it outright

## Who will host my website and will I be able to get access to the server?

It's important that you know who is hosting your site and that you have access to every part of its 'back end'. This usually means familiarity with several log-ins (user name and password); Administration, Control Panel, File Transfer Protocol (FTP), POP email accounts, etc. If the good relationship you have with your web developer breaks down you need to pass on access to their replacement to avoid downtime. Check the amount of time guaranteed for your website to be on line. It should not be less than 99.9%.

## Who will do my updates, how much will I be charged, and how quickly?

The site *can* be designed to allow you to make minor changes. Major updates are best done by the original designer but you need to ask how charges are calculated and how quickly they will do the work. It's not unusual for same day turnaround.

## Will my site validate according to W3C recommendations for both HTML and css?

Simple HTML errors can cause rendering problems for Internet browsers and the search engines. All errors are avoidable. You wouldn't employ anyone else who routinely made mistakes in other areas of the business.

## Will my site conform to the 1999 Disability Discrimination Act?

You definitely need this and your designer should know all about it. To read about your responsibilities in this important area go to www.webcredible.co.uk.

## Will my site work well in all the available browsers?

Remarkably, Microsoft's Internet Explorer (IE) is still the least accurate of all browsers despite being used by over 70% of Internet users. IE is gradually losing its dominance to alternatives like Firefox, Opera and Netscape,

## Will all of my content text be editable?

You need this but many designers, especially those who are more accustomed to designing for print, use image text instead of real text (that can be highlighted). Such text is invisible to blind people and search engines and should be avoided for anything other than decorative purposes. The same applies to Flash animation.

## Will I be able to preview my website as you're building it?

It is always a good idea to be able to preview your website as it is being developed, so avoiding any disappointment later. Your designer can upload it to a non-public address.

## Will my site be future-proof?

HTML is always developing, as are the ways that people view the Internet. It is important that your designer uses the latest versions of HTML (or XHTML) and that the site is viewable on a tiny hand-held device.

## Does your quotation include registration with the top free search engines and DMOZ?

If your site is new it should be manually registered with the top search engines and directories. If you have inbound links the search engines will find it anyway, but a listing in The Open Directory Project (www.dmoz.org), the largest human edited directory is a necessity.

## Will my site have a Flash or 'splash' page?

You don't need this! A 'splash' page is usually a very minimal or animated front page with a 'Click to Enter' link. Such pages are hugely unpopular with human visitors and are dreadful for successful results from search engines. Your front page should have between 200 to 250 real text words and navigation to most pages.

The BBC's website is regarded by many web site designers as 'the daddy' of them all. Certainly you'll find it one of the most complex on the web, but the designers have done a brilliant job of ensuring easy navigation with virtually instant access to a mass of information. It really is a supreme example of 'how to do it.' And there is no doubt of its origins either with a positive well known identity recognisable in every part of the site. Take your time browsing at www.bbc.co.uk.

*www.bbc.co.uk*

Conversely the 'OGOL' opening page - sometimes also wrongly referred to as a home page but more correctly termed 'entry page' - uses what is called a splash screen. You'll often see splash used in different guises on sites where a 'click to enter' message is displayed. Research has shown visitors tend not to linger too long on a splash entry page. This technique has the effect of demoting your home page (the one which should have all your essential information and important navigation links on it) to the second or third page that the user sees upon entering your site. Splash pages are also harder for search engines to find, since there are no key words to link on to.

*The wrong kind of opening page*

But don't take my word for it. Here is what Dr Jakob Nielsen, regarded by many as the guru of web site usability, has to say on his own website www.useit.com.

> "In reality, splash screens are annoying and users click off them as fast as they can. It is much better to design a single home page that unifies the situational identity message with a display of some useful news and directory information. Content itself can be used to tell users where they are and what the site is about."

## Will you be using Frames?

Most designers know that traditional HTML frames (where several pages are presented as one page) are bad news for blind people and search engines. It is possible to present similar effects with Cascading Style Sheets (CSS), Server

Side Includes (SSI) or Iframes and these are accessible to all. So you don't need frames!

## Will my site be a catalogue, a sales presentation for enquiries or a real online store?

Here's another instance of how knowing what you really want can set the scene for a successful website design from the outset.

You will need to know how much it's all going to cost of course and usually this will be broken down into several levels. Charges for website design and building are unfamiliar to most people so are best estimated specifically and alongside budgets laid down for the identity and subsequent items. Naturally the web design must be according to those foundations.

### The designer's initial fee

You should get a fixed quotation for a specific brief.

### Update costs

Will these be a fixed annual budget or by the hour?

### Hosting fees

This is the rent you pay for the server on which your website will live. Sometimes these will be included in the designer's fee; if not, you need to know how much you will be paying every year.

### Add-on costs

These include software such as shopping cart and Payment Gateway. The former is self-explanatory and is usually an annual cost. The latter is the company that processes the card transactions and payment is either monthly or annual.

## Domain costs

This is the name of your website e.g. mydomain.com. You may have several domains pointing to one website and usually they are payable biannually. You need to know who is responsible for paying these. It is always advisable to have them registered in your own name.

The answers you get from the above examples of questions to ask will give you a start on recognising how your designer is responding to the many and varied complexities of the World Wide Web. You should expect a confident, multi-faceted reply full of enthusiasm. Don't worry if it gets a bit technical. That's to be expected – in my experience, if it gets too technical to understand you're probably onto a winner!

# 9

# Briefing and working with your designer

You've talked to a few designers – now you have to choose just one to work with.

First, don't expect outstanding design to be done for free. In the world of big-budget advertising 'the competitive pitch', as it is sometimes called, is often done for nothing and without obligation. But winning an advertising account worth many thousands of pounds as the prize is not what we're about here, although unfortunately the practice is sometimes expected to rub off on designers because they're big-hearted folk and are perceived to be 'in the business'. In any event, you usually get what you pay for and putting several designers under pressure for free ideas so you can choose which one you think might suit you is hardly going to encourage their best efforts, is it? Encouraging people's best efforts is always a good policy to adopt for achieving successful results whatever the business.

Even after looking at impressive portfolios of stuff done for others, which never seem to exactly mirror what you have in mind, you'll still find it hard to know who to work with. A common error is to look for work done for similar businesses to yours in false hope of peace of mind thinking that they 'identify with your industry'. Conversely you might *not* want to see work for similar businesses to yours because you want a fresh approach to what the competition's already done. Keep an open opinion – just look for quality, ideas and enquiring minds.

Personalities count of course but you'll also need to be convinced about their professional capabilities, creative talents and that there is an understanding and empathy of what is going to be right for both you and your business.

Whatever indecisiveness you might feel, it isn't fair to ask for work to be done for nothing with a challenge of 'Let's see what you can do then and if I like what I see you'll get paid.' Remember that from a designer's point of view you may be seen as an unknown quantity unused to appreciating how much time goes into creative work – they will be particularly keen to establish your ability, and willingness, to pay bills promptly! This is a business deal and despite the artistic links, there are not many designers around with ambitions to die penniless in a barely furnished garret!

Ideas scribbled out over lunch on the back of an envelope are also unlikely to give you the carefully considered thinking you want either. If they desperately need work you may get away with some free ideas, but this is taking an unfair advantage of a situation and doesn't lead to a satisfactory and trusting long term relationship. In any event it may pay to ask yourself why their order book appears to be bereft of happy, contented clients.

However, I believe it is fair to ask for initial ideas without cost on how your project would be *approached*. Discuss budgets informally, agree what's to be done in broad terms, and get to know their fee or payment structure. How much time could you expect them to spend together with you against your budget, and how much do they think you might be required to spend not only on initial design and production work, but also ongoing implementation. For example will they be remunerated in part by buying print or advertising space on your behalf, and if so how much will this be marked up? Will they be paid by publisher's commission alone on space? They may prefer to project manage such aspects on a fee basis and charge you net – then everyone knows exactly where they stand without hidden agendas.

At last, you've found your designer! Now comes the difficult – and the fun – bit.

Eventually (the earlier the better) you will have to give a clear brief to your designers, so here's how to write – or have a handle on a design brief. A good brief minimises risk of confusion and it helps to save later arguments if you provide this in written form. Alternatively you can pay your chosen designers for an outline proposal report written against your verbal brief. This will show if they've understood what you've said to them and give you the opportunity to evaluate their abilities and ideas of approach at an early stage before committing funds to visuals and creative work.

A short outline report is sometimes offered on a speculative basis but don't anticipate an in-depth evaluation with comprehensive cost estimates, schedules and creative platforms ready for development.

Whether you're writing a design brief or giving one orally, all parties should be clear on what it sets out to achieve. This may sound obvious but it is easy inadvertently to latch on to ideas which have been done before and which are perceived as being successful (by a competitor perhaps), and adapt those ideas to fit your needs. Don't!

I remember when as a young man employed by a design agency I was told by the marketing director of a bakery company that we were working with to go to the local supermarket to see what their competitors' packaging was like. Because these packs had proved to be a selling success he asked me to note all the good points and incorporate them into the new range of packs we were designing. That, he said, would provide the results he wanted, and if we really wanted a design brief from him, that was it. It seemed he wanted his packaging to match and blend in!

Well, things have moved on a bit from those days and whilst it is unquestionably a good idea to know what your competition is up to, copying their principles of design is no way to differentiate yourself in the marketplace or make a positive visual statement about your product or services which in turn creates motivation to buy from you, not them.

It's the same with your design brief. Make sure it's uniquely yours. On the whole, my opinion is that you must make the brief factual, and your mantra of 'knowing what you really want' comes across clearly. In other words, don't try to pre-empt the answers to the questions and objectives raised in the brief in an attempt to be helpful. It is a briefing and not a report after all. Keep it open-ended with opportunities for others to contribute ideas on 'what you really want' and to respond on a broader front than you may have imagined yourself. You need to allow freedom for creative proposals within the extents you have laid down. How your designers interpret this will be their test.

OK, what must the brief contain and is there a recognised format to follow?

The short answer is as much relevant information as you can think of, and no, there is not an industry standard format to follow. It helps also to get agreement from your colleagues on what's included in the brief, but don't let too many people obscure issues with over-complicated views. Waiting until the design visual stage to resolve differences in opinion on what the organisation needs simply gets expensive. Just make sure your brief is comprehensible and concise when it eventually reaches your designer and you won't have to spend more than you need – hopefully!

As a guide, here's a structure you may like to follow.

1. The Current Situation
2. Your market – who you are trying to reach
3. Budgets and schedules

Begin with **'The Current Situation'**.

Put in plain words the background to your business, its history and its aspirations, and summarise the marketplace in which it operates. Don't assume your designer knows anything about your industry or business sector.

Explain the financial aspects of your business – nothing confidential obviously – but it helps at the outset to impart a little confidence to your design team so they won't feel there's any likelihood of finding themselves out of pocket. This may seem strange to honest folk like you, but unfortunately, and linked to the practice of 'pitching for free', the undesirable bad debt crops up with surprising frequency in designers' new business situations.

If you are already up and running as a business, show them examples of all the visual materials you've produced to date. I trust you'll already have assembled these items when carrying out the exercise in the earlier chapter suggesting how to find out what your firm looks like, so it shouldn't be too much of a hassle. You did, didn't you?

Explain the thinking behind these materials – say what you think is good about them, and what may not be so good, and explain why you are seeking to make changes. Explain how the position is going to be affected by future plans. Make sure you include everything used in day-to-day running of the business: invoices; letterheads; receipts; any off-the-shelf stationery; ads you may have run; photographs of your building and sign written vehicles; promotional material; exhibitions or shows you have attended in the past two years.

Even if you think the current materials are failing completely, make sure you explain why you originally thought they would be successful. You must have felt what you produced earlier to have been a good idea at the time, and your original thinking will give designers a crucial insight into what you are trying to achieve. It might turn out to be only the manifestation or implementation of what you're using which is wrong – do you already have good, recognisable visual elements which are being misused? Or it could simply be that you have moved on a bit? Is it a good idea to retain any of these existing visual elements? After all, regular customers recognise you for what you are, warts and all. You won't know the answers yet. What I am driving at is an attempt to get the whole picture established early and laid out so everyone understands where you're at, where you're coming from, and where you hope to be.

If you're working to a mission statement, now is the time to make it known.

You haven't got a mission statement? Some may scoff at such things, but they can help to focus everyone's mind on what the firm is all about and work as a reminder for both objectives and the attitudes staff are expected to adopt.

If you're going to invent a mission statement, it should be simple and to the point. One of my personal favourites and most succinct given the vastness of the operation is from search engine Google:

> *Google mission statement:*
> *"To organise the world's information and make it universally accessible and useful."*

Good, isn't it?

The second part of your design brief is about **'Your market – who you are trying to reach'**.

You have already summarised the marketplace in which you operate but will this hold true for future planning? Tell the design team if the identity should seek to consolidate perceptions held by your existing customer base or attract wider interest from within the same sector. Outline any other markets which are to be targeted in future. Demographic facts about your customers also help to focus design thinking.

Is the design required to support an aggressive sales policy by possessing colourful impact; or solicit serious enquiries by way of subtle understated graphics; or encourage gathering of information using an official format style? Permutations are endless, of course, and again only you can decide what you really want. It helps – although I'm on slightly dodgy ground here – if you express personal preferences. Try not to be too dominant, but impart a few clues as to what you think will appeal to your market and fit comfortably with your own tastes. Leaving an entirely open and ill-defined stage upon which your designer is expected to perform doesn't often work perfectly and leads to unnecessary delays and expense while they 'get it right'. On the other hand, an open and ill-defined stage can result in some surprising ideas and inspired thinking about what the designer feels is what you really want.

Illustrate the visual status of your market by including a few examples of material produced by competitors alongside designs from elsewhere that impress you for one reason or another. Discuss these paradigms with your designers, not for them to copy ideas (and please remember my earlier experience with the Bakery) but more to kick-start the design process on a positive note. It all helps to profile the market and ensure your solutions stand out.

The final part of the brief is very important – **'Budgets and schedules'**.

When it comes to money there are invariably many different attitudes expressed by clients across all kinds of businesses, but a recurring suspicion is that if designers know what a budget is they'll make damn sure they spend it all. There may be some unscrupulous operators out there (aren't there always!) but if you've followed my guidance and chosen a professional design team there is never a problem revealing all about your budget plans. Contrary to provoking a problem it helps enormously and saves time and frustration in arriving at a right solution. (Do you recall the 'right' and 'wrong' ways referred to in the opening section 'Read this first'?)

Challenges such as 'We haven't got anything much to spend so just come up with a few ideas and then if we like them we'll give you the full story,' or 'Show us what you can do and we'll see if we can find the money,' won't work any oracles. Written down like that I'm sure you can see the folly of such unprofessional tactics, but it does happen – it's happened to me. Not only is it unprofessional, it's unfair too. Look upon the design team as an intrinsic part of your organisation, build mutual trust, and lay down foundations for a long-term working relationship and you won't go far wrong.

For designers to successfully work within a budget means they not only need to know what money is available for initial creation of ideas for a programme, but must also be aware of budgets for ongoing production costs, printing, and subsequent implementation of every element of identity throughout the business. It is essential that design solutions are tailored to meet future plans and that means knowing the full story on budgets.

Schedules, too, can be rendered unrealistic by wasting time on design efforts resulting from misguided budget information. Make sure you discuss schedules at the outset, get to understand the time it takes for sometimes complex processes to happen and leave sufficient margins for the things that go wrong and delay delivery. Co-ordinating different media and arranging for separate items to magically appear together on a particular launch day, for example, often involves wildly varying lead times.

On the other hand, assuming you've chosen a switched-on design team, they will frequently exploit the wonders of modern technology to produce things at a speed which may pleasantly you – but that's no excuse for you not to plan for the unforeseen!

So is that it, then? The brief as simple as that? In a word, Yes. All the information your designers will need to respond proactively with ideas and a presentation to knock you sideways and your firm well into next week.

**Presentation Day** has arrived. The day when you finally get to see the results of all your hard work sifting and shortlisting, digging out facts for the brief, and conveying your thoughts on what you really want. It's an exciting day for designers too, who generally find they look forward to it full of confidence and enthusiasm, mingled with a tinge of apprehension speculating on your response to the brilliance of their ideas.

I say Presentation Day because that is really what it should be. You may hear of a plan to send your designs as an attachment to an email and whilst this may be OK for subsequent design amendments and additions in day-to-day implementation, it is definitely *not* OK to email this crucially important inaugural design work. The same goes for computer presentations of graphics. In my opinion you simply do not get the right *feel* for the designs on a computer screen; nor can one spread out visuals to gain a true impression of what your new identity is adding up to.

So what should you be looking for in your designer's presentation? It is often seen as the bane of designers' lives that standards of quality and creativity are seen and immediately judged by those without much experience or any formal qualifications in the subject whatsoever! In design and advertising circles this kind of appraisal is disparagingly known as the 'ATCS' syndrome – Ask The Chairperson's Spouse! This may come over as a little cynical and disrespectful, especially as you are paying the bill, and in reality you will know instinctively if the ideas being presented are going to materialise as some of those 'right' solutions.

Nevertheless, don't be surprised if any hasty criticisms you may make are met with a certain degree of resistance and defensive expressions. Artistic temperament can prevail on such occasions and it may be helpful for you to keep in mind that the presentation is most probably the result of much heart-searching and debate by people who regard their latest designs as masterpieces in their own right, destined for awards and recognition by peers the world over. Of course, I am being flippant here, but be aware that decisions here can be taken personally if not handled with care and tact.

Assuming then that you have opted to see visuals in conventional layout form, I have always believed it to be good practice to summarise and discuss the essential elements of the brief, and to establish how these have been interpreted *before* everyone in the meeting gets too distracted by opening a portfolio and looking at pictures. This gives you the opportunity to quiz the designers and ask them to explain how their conclusions have been reached, so helping your ensuing deliberations to be guided along the same tracks.

Let the presentation run its course. Watch carefully, listen and evaluate all that's being said before commenting and passing initial judgement. Remember a good idea is infinitely more valuable than any highly finished visuals packaged simply to make that idea look superficially impressive. That said, any designer worth their salt will go to great lengths to make the most of an idea and it's down to you to look beyond and recognise the long-term stamina of that idea and know that it really *is* what you want for your identity. Remember that decisions on identity will be commitments supporting and promoting your firm for a long time.

Your objective in this process is to find that one good idea which will drive all aspects of your business promotion. The singularity is important. Even if the visuals incorporate *many* lively ideas demonstrating how your new identity might be developed, it is still essential for 'the big idea' to be clear and easily understood. Watch for this.

Make a note of the paper being specified for literature, and especially your stationery. It often pays to use a better quality stock for 'ambassadorial' items such as letterheads and compliment slips which are seen most often by customers, and then to economise on supporting paraphernalia by using a more standard stock. 'Better quality' paper stock inevitably means 'more expensive', but you might well enjoy the pleasure of additional prestige it brings together with introducing an element of exclusivity. There is a wonderful choice of paper out there and sample sheets should be made available along with visuals for you to browse through. If there are no samples to evaluate, your designer has fallen down on the presentation.

When the bolts have all been shot, as it were, do not feel pressure to react immediately. You might want to jump up and down in a state of euphoria, of course, but it is quite normal for a brief period of quietness to descend on the meeting waiting for your deliberations and the questions which inevitably arise. Certainly your designer will be hanging on every word at this point and may be tempted to break the stillness with some form of reassuring words to back up what has been said.

I remember with some amusement (not at the time) an occasion when at this pregnant quiet time at the end of what turned out to be a highly successful presentation for a large international client, my colleague, unable to contain the suspense of the moment, blurted out: 'Of course it's not there yet, but if you like it, we'll get it right.'

---

*Tip*

**Don't expect design work for free, and look beyond the glitz of the presentation to get value for money.**

---

# 10

# How to reach the people who might want to buy from you

What should you watch out for?

The opportunities are virtually endless. It's not really a matter of *exactly* how you reach those people, more of deciding on the most relevant and effective tactics to employ which give the best value for money, fall affordably within your budget, and promote the firm in an environment relevant to all the principles laid down by your identity programme. Let's take an informal, uncomplicated look at some of the more obvious alternatives at your disposal.

## Advertisements

Ah, here's the bit where everybody is an expert. Have you ever met anyone who hasn't passed an opinion on an advertisement? Perhaps if we narrowed that person's opinion down more precisely we may discover they're referring to a particular television commercial which has taken their fancy, even if the advertiser's name or product cannot be remembered! Certainly, whenever advertising is discussed socially, you'll find it's generally television in the firing line and rarely newspapers or magazines, let alone the broader aspects of advertising and promotion. This can be discouraging for the smaller business. Because you won't be spending millions on television, people won't notice any other form of advertising. So there's no point advertising anywhere unless you're on TV. Right?

Of course I'm not right. Even though not many people bother to comment on advertisements they see everyday, it doesn't mean to say your customers and potential buyers are not being influenced or persuaded to buy. Advertising works – and works well if done properly. There's absolutely no doubt of that.

There is a general misconception about how advertising expenditure is divided between the different media. Many people think television accounts for the lion's share. They may be interested to learn that recent figures for the UK published by the Advertising Association show over 43% of expenditure in press advertising with television accounting for just 24%. However, when classified advertising is discounted and display advertising only is considered (the sort which carries your identity) positions are reversed with press at 32% and television 34%. If you'd like to know how much cash these figures represent, think around £19 billion when spending on direct mail, outdoor, radio, internet and cinema is included. You can see the latest statistics on the AA's website at www.adassoc.org.uk.

You will probably have heard the well-known adage about advertising attributed to the first Lord Leverhulme: as he famously said, you know half of your money is being wasted, but you're never sure which half. Personally, I do not wholly agree with that view inasmuch as every time your firm's name is associated with a service or product and seen as part of a corporate identity programme your presence in the marketplace grows. In that sense it matters not one jot whether 100% of readers are influenced or persuaded specifically to buy or respond to you at that point. So no, half your money is not wasted – let's say just invested for later.

The actual creation of an advertisement or a campaign is always going to be highly subjective whatever you do, and you'll have to rely on your own good judgement and the abilities of your designer and copywriter when evaluating visual appeal and likely effectiveness, whether this means raising general awareness, changing attitudes to the brand, selling directly off the page or generating leads. One thing certain, however, is that you must look for coherent thinking where both message and the visual compliment each other. It is no good whatever having a beautifully designed ad with a boring headline and text, or conversely clever words and a static layout. By the way, whatever the purpose of your advertisement of the day is, you will ensure it all fits in to the corporate identity and the visual standards you have laboured so long to establish, won't you?

How do you know if an ad is a good one? Apart from considerations of aesthetic appeal and response levels, it's the one that is most visible. In the example illustrated below, a local newspaper is running two ads for the same company, Climax Windows, on the front page. See which one you see first! I hope it's the "Earpiece" ad with the prominent logo, demonstrating that position and clear functional layout has more to do with being noticed than a larger, relatively indistinct ad in full colour.

*Climax Windows advertisements*

You often see a good ad spoilt by bad words. Even the big guns get it wrong sometimes. In the following example from a leading insurance company, the message itself is very strong. The layout is crisp, clean and prominent, successfully upholding the prestigiousness of their corporate identity. The gaff in my opinion, is the grammatical error in the headline. Surely 'fees' should be singular or alternatively 'There are no admin fees'? The error is further compounded by using both 'fee' and 'fees' in the text. What do they mean? Is there only one fee, or several they don't charge?

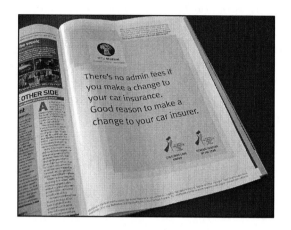

*An ad which was not proofread!*

You may like to make a special note of remembering what is written about checking copy in Chapter Ten, including *"get someone else to proofread and check grammar."*

The 'Berl' ad on page 69 is a good example of how strong use of photography with a direct headline which means something relevant in a specialist market, can work in black and white. It also means achieving the impact of a full page ad at similar, or less cost, than a smaller colour ad.

Remember, when you're trying to reach the reader of your ad, that they will be looking at your proposition from an entirely different viewpoint from your own. You must try to find out what this is. They may be entirely logical in what they perceive, but their logic may have a different basis from your own. By way of illustration, imagine yourself walking along a river. You see someone on the opposite bank and shout, "How can I get to the other side?" They hesitate and shout back, "You ARE on the other side."

*Use of photography in advertisements*

In my final illustration, on page 70, see how thinking "out of the box" resulted in a surprisingly effective advertising campaign for a leading supplier of stainless steel. Unusually for such an industrialised specialist product, a much softer approach in black and white using a theme of nature and environment as a background proved to be highly successful both in terms of response levels and favourable comment from an established customer base. It shows you don't always have to follow the accepted style of an industry!

# BAR FROM CASHMORES— THE NATURAL CHOICE

Stainless steel bar stockholding might sound like a straightforward downstream sort of business. And up to a point it is.

So long as you remember that to be successful in the highly competitive world of stainless steel stockholding you need to offer much more than just material in a warehouse.

You need to have the right material in stock. At the right time. At the right price. You need resources to give technical advice and massive financial investment to make sure your customers' requirements are delivered quickly and reliably without fuss or bother – wherever they are situated. Whatever the size of their order.

And if you can accomplish all these things in a friendly style with total commitment from experienced people you'll discover a stockholder of natural ability.

Just like Cashmores Stainless!

## Cashmores Stainless

STAINLESS STEEL SHEET · STRIP · PLATE · BAR · TUBE · PIPE · FITTINGS AND FASTENERS

**Headquarters and Warehouse**
Upper Brook Street
Walsall
WS2 9PD

**Midlands**
Tel: (0922) 720930
Telex: 338879
Fax: (0922) 648304

**Scotland**
Tel: 041-637 0269
Telex: 338879

**North**
Tel: 061-962 7111
Telex: 668763
Fax: 061-973 6132

**Wales and the South West**
Tel: (0633) 252101
Telex: 498248
Fax: (0633) 211878

**London and the South East**
Tel: (0753) 682921
Telex: 848177
Fax: (0753) 686018

*Thinking outside the box*

Earlier I dismissed ideas scribbled out over lunch on the back of an envelope as probably not being able to pull off that vital sparkling design solution required for a successful corporate identity. When it comes to advertisements, perhaps I need to moderate that statement somewhat, because often a brilliant idea just happens out of the blue. It can happen at any time to any individual working on your project and there seems to be no logical explanation for this. A brilliant idea for an advertisement has no need for a flashy, highly-finished visual to make it look as though it will work. In the same way you looked for the idea in the presentation of your identity, you must also look for it in advertisement terms. There is no substitute for an idea. Just make sure it's an original one that works not only for what you want to communicate in that particular advertisement, but also to direct the reader's selection of response. A succession of good ideas running as a campaign will also redefine your competitive edge and with a bit of luck relegate the opposition to a state of trembling jellies! If you can achieve all this and surprise your audience as well, you'll have a good advertisement.

## Copy-writing

Unless you have appointed a full service advertising agency, it is unlikely that your graphics designer will have the necessary talents or resource to write convincing copy. Headlines and visual ideas yes, but easy-reading relevant copy is a function of an advertisement requiring both specialist skills and experience. It's why you'll usually find a team of Art Director, Designer and Copy-writer assigned to clients in larger advertising agencies. However the absence of such an in-house team at your designer agency need not be a problem if freelance copy-writers are available. I would suggest you meet the writer along with your designer at the earliest opportunity and insist upon personal access to them throughout the creation of your of advertising campaign. Discussing someone else's copy ideas through a third party never works.

Here are ten basic techniques to help you have an informed dialogue with the creators of your advertisement:

1.  Ensure that everything produced, every word written and every layout created is consistent and complies with the principles of your corporate identity.

2.  Communicate the message. This requirement may be obvious but always look closely – *really* closely – at what you are saying. State clearly what you have for sale. Offer a benefit. Can it be misread or misunderstood? Many potential customers have never heard of you before and may care even less about what you have to sell them right now. Then again, they may care a lot if they want what you're selling and are unable to find it elsewhere. Make sure they understand what you want to say to them.

3.  Don't try to be *too* clever with headlines. Competition for attention is merciless and it's easy to try too hard and end up with inappropriate meanings. Show your firm out of context, twist words around and be innovative, certainly, but avoid 'gaffes' that can be misread. For example. 'Don't buy a used car elsewhere and get ripped off – come here instead.'

4.  Keep the idea clean and direct. Aim to create a good first impression, and avoid clutter with too many messages needing text copy in small type and over-complicated visual elements. It's a mistake to illustrate the headline. Many amateurs do it in an attempt to clarify a statement but this just leads to confusion. Illustrate the idea of what you're selling and let that simply complement the headline.

5.  Remember that visual impact is noticed first (this applies to either headline, illustration or both of them working together). Catch the reader's eye and get your main point and the benefits you offer over *fast*.

6.  Make sure your advertisement speaks quality all the way, and keep your meaning clear. Blurred photographs and spelling misteaks do not help to give confidence in what your ad is saying. Similarly, get someone else to proof-read and check grammar. A second eye always sees things you don't. Some may not think grammar is important in a promotional message but it is, and even big names sometimes get it wrong. Consider, for example, the ubiquitous supermarket checkout posters labelled 'ten items or less' instead of the correct 'ten items or fewer'? A technical distinction, I know, but wrong nevertheless, as any GCSE English teacher

will explain. Good grammar and punctuation will be more persuasive and is a key element in presenting your message effectively. Sadly, not many people bother about such misuse of English or even know what's right, but everywhere you go you can witness examples of bad grammar and words wrongly spelt, and there will always be *someone* who notices – and that someone may be just the person you are trying to reach! It's very easy to make errors and indeed sit in judgement of others, and whilst I've tried to use correct form in this book I know there will be many instances where my writing should be better to make meanings clearer. Any comments gratefully received!

7. Check out and avoid any likely problems with copy if you think it might infer ageism, be sexist, or have political, religious, or racist overtones. Such matters can be quite subtle and easily missed.

8. Know who you are selling to, and define the solution you are offering. Don't let your ad try to solve a problem the reader doesn't have. Maybe there's no problem of paint dripping; all that is wanted is a freshly decorated front room!

9. Whether it's a one-off advertisement or a campaign, keep both your copy-writing and visual styles consistent and you'll build a stronger perception of the firm in the media which adds strength to the values of your corporate identity.

10. Ask the reader to take action, or at least guide them towards making a response. Make sure you include an admonition to buy, telephone, navigate to your website, respond by coupon, or visit your dealer. Involve the reader. Keep them on your side and avoid the faintest hint of self-importance or arrogance.

## Placement

Deciding where to place your advertisement if you are to achieve maximum effectiveness is an art in itself – some would say a black art! Unless yours is a localised business where it's really pretty obvious which media to use, you would be well advised to consult either a media buyer or an advertising agency who will be able to offer the benefits of their wide experience. With the plethora of newspapers and magazines at your disposal, it takes practical knowledge and up-to-date information at one's fingertips to know which ones are best. It is unlikely that your design team will have the necessary expertise and will need to call on specialist help from a third party in any case. They usually have contacts or can suggest independent media planners who you can talk to personally. In any event, I think you would find such a meeting invaluable.

Undoubtedly, you will be bombarded by publishers' representatives and telephone sales enthusiasts all willing to take your money with unprecedented bargains and opportunities not to be missed. Do not be taken in with such offers. Stick to your media spending plan and leave yourself the benefit of measuring the effectiveness of your advertising over a fixed period. If you're not careful, the 'bargains and opportunities' will end up costing a lot more money than the original campaign, and risk being seen in inappropriate places at the wrong time. Plan on your terms – not the publishers' terms!

One day I was contacted for help by a man owning a wonderful eighteenth century coaching inn which served excellent food. Unfortunately the eating side of the business was under-performing, and in an attempt to address this he had been taking advantage of every opportunity to appear in 'Eating out' features offered by various local newspapers and magazines. At the time this was the only advertising he did, always appearing (or getting lost depending how you look at it) amongst competitors in the area and consequently seen as just another pub. The advertising had made no discernible difference to the number of customers coming through the door and trade remained static. The answer was straightforward. Re-brand with a new identity and redirect the cash spent on feature advertising with a controlled programme of regular small space ads to promote the new image and keep the name of the pub constantly in front of customers. To launch the identity the campaign also included local press PR and a leaflet drop. Within four months of adopting this tactic the restaurant business had taken off and had even created a waiting list for tables.

The project was a rewarding demonstration of how planning on your terms and not the publishers' terms can trigger success – and it doesn't need big budgets to work in your favour.

Another aspect you'll need to think about when planning is that of wastage. Why pay for an advertisement at a price based on full circulation of a journal or newspaper if many of its readers have no need for your product? It all depends, of course, on what you're selling and whether local, national or specialist trade media are required. You may like to think about alternatives, however, such as special regional editions or specific titles targeted within your area of business.

Also important is the question of the number frequency of advertisement repeats, and, of course, the size of ad. Check out readership profiles carefully before committing. The publishers will have all the data to hand if you ask.

Beware the magazine that invites you (along with others) to pay for an advertisement in support of a special feature promoting one of your customers. This form of revenue generation by publishers is ethically questionable at best. These features have little value to either the customer or to you, and it is unlikely to affect relationships either way if you decline the invitation.

Conversely, if a 'free' feature is offered to you I recommend refusal as you will undoubtedly be asked for a list of your customers and suppliers who can be approached to 'support' *you*. Depending on the level of response, the size of the feature will be adjusted accordingly. The only dubious winner is the publisher. This reveals again why it's better to plan media expenditure on your terms and not the publishers' terms.

You may think from the above that I don't much like publishers. I have to confess that I do. I love the enthusiasm of media representatives and their willingness to strike a deal wherever they can, and to share gossip about the trade. Your trade. Get to know these people, invest a little time and understand how they operate. When you've a friendly and open working relationship you'll discover an ongoing wealth of knowledge and helpfulness which can be invaluable. You can often save money on the authorised rates, secure better positioning, and if you have stretch a deadline to the absolute limit you'll get inside assistance to operate every dodge in the book!

I am unable to express similar enthusiasm for the telephone sales executives a.k.a. media representatives who offer unprecedented bargains for space in publications you may not even have heard of. Stick with those you know and plan on your terms.

There was an interesting discussion I once had following an ad I placed to sell my car. On offer from one of these telephone sales guys from a rival publication was a sure path to an immediate sale. He said I had used the wrong paper for my ad and if I used his instead over 200,000 buyers would be queuing at my door. That was the newspaper's circulation but how many of his readers were car buyers? That was a question he could not answer of course. So, be wary of statistics thrown at you and question what they really mean in practice.

# Directories

Should advertisements in directories be a part of your corporate identity? Hmm, slightly knotty question to answer here, because it is possible to spend all of your budget money on directory advertisements which in comparison to other media appear to promise an unrivalled number of enquiries for the same outlay. The people who sell space in directories routinely claim you will get better value for money, and in some circumstances they may be right. However, I would never recommend relying solely on directories rather than more broad-based advertising to foster your identity, if only because there is such a veritable mass and mess of advertisements which effectively mask your firm, even if your ad does follow style. On the other hand, directories can be important to you.

One of my clients felt the only form of press advertising he should have must be in directories, since the prime requirement was for enquiries from the general public specifically looking for the range of domestic products he offered. There is some logic in this argument, but when faced with pages full of advertisers all selling apparently identical products, would you choose to contact someone you'd never heard of before, or a familiar company whose name you recognise?

I suggest a directory presence always needs endorsement to work properly, and with support from an identity tightly controlled and visible across other promotional activities, it will have a higher prospect of success.

So whether or not directory advertisements should be a part of your corporate identity has to be left in the air a little. It all depends on individual circumstances.

There is a point of view suggesting that if a firm provides outstanding quality in everything it does at a competitive price it will have little need to have advertisements in any kind of press. Perhaps – but how will new customers be found? How will new products be introduced? How will identity be broadcast to a wider field? How will market share be expanded?

It is true to say that press advertising is not for all firms, on every occasion, but do not discard it without careful consideration. As stated earlier, it is crucial to maintain constant vigilance on your options.

## Some of the jargon you'll come across

The publishing world is full of jargon and abbreviated descriptions. You need to know your way around these to be able to talk convincingly with your professional advisors. There are many in use, covering a bewildering array of different combinations, specifications, position and sizes of advertisements. Some of the more general terms you'll come across include:

- **ROP** – Run of paper. This means your ad will appear anywhere in the newspaper the publisher thinks fit.

- **FM** – Facing matter. You pay for your ad to appear on a page facing or surrounded by text.

- **Bleed Page** – Your ad is not restricted to the publication's 'type area' but covers the whole page to the trimmed edges, and therefore needs to include a bit of printed area or 'bleed' outside the actual trimmed edges to allow for variations in trim position and avoid white edges. (The 'type area' is the fixed box of text on a page surrounded on all four sides by margins.)

- **B&W** – Your ad appears printed in black (no colour).

- **2 col** – Either (1) your ad appears printed in black plus one of the standard colours used in the rest of the publication, usually Red or Blue, but can be Yellow or (2) your ad will be two column widths wide. Column widths are the measurements of a publication's standard typesetting, which, just to confuse you, can vary on different pages and always between different publications. There are no universally standard column widths. Column widths generally refer to newspapers and the term 'ten across two' means your ad will be ten centimetres deep by two columns wide. Similarly fifteen across three means – well, you know...

- **Full page, Half page, Quarter page, One-eighth page** – Most magazines use these terms to denote standard ad sizes rather than column widths.

- **OFC, IFC, IBC, OBC** – These refer to positions of your ad in a magazine: Outside front cover, Inside front cover, Inside back cover and Outside back cover respectively.

- **Solus** – You pay for your ad to be the only one on the page, usually in a newspaper.

- **DPS** – Double page spread. Your advertisement takes up two full pages and usually means you'll have bleed sizes thrown in.

- **Earpiece** – The small space ad on the front page of a newspaper beside the masthead, or name of the paper. However, small ads on the back page can also be called earpieces.

- **Four colour half tone or 4 col h/t** – Means full colour reproduction, and therefore you can use colour photographs along with colour text exactly as you wish. However, these days it is more usual to refer to such ads simply as 'full colour'.

Just before we leave the subject of advertising, you will make sure, won't you, that wherever you choose to place your ad, the claims you make for your product or service comply with the Code of Advertising Practice regulations. The same applies, of course, to any promotion you undertake including direct mail and literature. The regulations are fairly straightforward, and as long as your advertisement is legal, decent, truthful and honest, you usually won't have anything to worry about.

You can check out these regulations at www.cap.org.uk.

> *Tip*
>
> If you are in to press advertising remember it's the idea
> for the advertisement that is infinitely more valuable
> than anything else, and insist your media planning is on
> your own terms.

# Promotions

The expression 'promotion' means different things to different people. Some use the word promotion to mean advertising or advertisements in a general sense, while others intend it to mean an offer of some description, or a 'deal'. Usually from a company perspective it will mean a combination of things scheduled to happen over a fixed time: advertisements; leaflet distribution; direct mail; money off; dealer's or sales person's incentives and so on.

For the purpose of this section, I am referring to special offers. With this use of the word, the most successful promotions are carried on the back of an established form where a firm is recognised and perceived to be all the things we've explored earlier in the book. Under pressure from the very nature of promotions demanding that extra element of pushiness, there is invariably temptation to depart from those strict rules of consistency and end up as a short-term fix for the task in hand with promotional material possessing little or no relevance to your identity. That's both money and an opportunity wasted.

There is, however, a significant ray of hope here in the examples you can see demonstrated by leading retail companies, especially department stores, of how promotions work successfully as part of a corporate identity programme. I urge you to look out for these paradigms of the hard sell. If it works for them; it can work for you too. They are proof that you really do not have to use risky, garish material to make your offer irresistible.

# Literature

Corporate literature includes brochures, reports and accounts, and promotional leaflets of varying kinds. Some people regard corporate literature as a necessary evil, particularly the report and accounts! However, this understates its function. The production of all kinds of printed materials is an exciting sphere where you can 'play tunes' with your identity design. You must make certain whatever literature you have is clearly understood as being part of the identity plan, obviously, but there are many opportunities to make your business shine and dazzle the reader with innovative invitations to attract business; or to consolidate it with information clearly laid out. The publication of corporate literature is an opportunity for your firm to 'dress up' – not, of course, in fancy dress where individuals cannot be recognised, but more a matter of getting all dressed up with somewhere to go, make an impression and captivate an audience.

I'm referring here to more than just sales literature. Whatever printed items your customers see, they all have to be produced to strict specifications to meet the same high standards of presentation. These 'high standards' do not necessarily involve high costs – paper stocks, for example, should be tailored to the needs of the specific function – but must involve high standards of design consistent with your identity principles, rules of typography and copy-writing style. Data sheets, Instruction leaflets, Technical specification flyers, and Price Lists, to name but four typical areas of print, all need to come under your literature wing and be controlled as such.

Before we launch into looking at some of these exciting design directions, what pitfalls might be lurking and waiting to catch you out? It is easy to concentrate on the creative aspect of design work and ignore the logistical side, but production logistics hold many pitfalls for the unwary. Casting a wary eye can help you to avoid unwanted hassle, and curb any rash decisions on design matters just to meet a deadline. It can happen. Anyway, if you have a good designer you should be able to avoid most of these potential hazards and production hang-ups at the outset.

Late or frantic last-minute deliveries are one of the most common pitfalls. Such problems often arise because one small detail is unavailable when all the other artwork, or origination, has been completed in good time. Perhaps a supplier has not provided a promised photograph, or results from a test lab or field trial are awaited, or simply someone forgot to pass on an amendment to a price. Silly things in isolation, and so easily avoided if you plan and allow enough time. A printer is unable to do anything until every last detail is in place. It's simply not physically possible to get on and make film or plates and then add in a bit when you're ready. Similarly, if you change your mind about something and amendments are made at printer's proof stage, costs will be incurred which could have been avoided. It's relatively easy to make changes to artwork but when new reproduction film and plates have to be made to accommodate changes, however tiny those changes may be, someone has to pay for them. That'll be you, then.

Sometimes 'computer to plate' technology may be employed and the proofs you see will be generated digitally, in which case amendments are more easily executed, but you can still get charged.

It's wise to remember that whatever proofs you see, the colours will be slightly different on the final printed sheets, and if colour reproduction is a critical issue, get to see the job off the printing press itself as it is running.

Make sure you check and proofread your copy at typescript stage before it goes to your designer's studio. Then check it again on artwork. Then check it again on proofs. However carefully one checks copy, mistakes can and do happen. Who has never missed a spelling mistake? Not me, for one! My most monumental error was when I worked with an advertising agency connected with the launch of a new super industrial compressor for a client I shall call Blot. We created a brand logo in an expanded typeface to appear in the launch advertisements covering both trade and local press, on a big exhibition stand featuring the new compressor, in sales literature, direct mail and display material for distributors throughout the country. The logo read – in expanded letters remember – *'The new super industrial compessor from Blot'*. It appeared everywhere and the launch was deemed to be highly successful for all concerned.

Six months later the Managing Director of Blot received a call from one of his distributors in the North. 'Hey. I'm sat here in my showroom looking at your poster,' said the distributor. 'Did you know you've spelt compressor wrong?'

Everybody, from the MD to marketing assistants at Blot, through the agency's studio personnel, secretaries, account handlers and director, printers reps and advertising departments of numerous magazine and newspapers, and of course myself, had missed the error which now of course was blatantly obvious on so many items. To their credit, Blot were really very phlegmatic about it all, but it was an object lesson for me – and demonstrates how things can escalate by the absence of one small letter on a design visual. Because that is where the original error occurred.

---

*Tip*

**Check copy. Check copy. Then check again.**

---

Lateness of copy and missed spelling errors are certainly amongst the most common pitfalls you'll stumble over, but there are a couple more aspects to watch for when checking out proofs.

Naturally, you will be checking for colour accuracy, but as we've already noted, colour does tend to vary on the print run itself.

Chunks of content can go awol between the design studio's computer and the proofing press. This is surprisingly regular occurrence even on digital proofs, which in theory should be immune to such failings.

A photograph can mysteriously appear upside down, or the wrong way round because someone has laid down a transparency in reverse.

You will usually be looking at colour proofs in flat sheet form so if it's a brochure of more than four pages, make sure you also see a full size dummy made up to ensure pagination is correct.

```
                          Tip
    Check copy. Check that all contents are on proofs.
                    Then check again.
```

## The words

The words you use in your literature are obviously of critical importance. Many of the principles used to create copy for an advertisement can also be applied to corporate literature (see 'Copy-writing' on page 71). Primarily you should decide who you want to read it and then target content accordingly. Sounds obvious? How often have you received literature you haven't bothered to read? Would that have been because its contents were of no interest, or because it did not look attractive, or was full of technical terminology and difficult to understand? For example, a technical leaflet might be written by a product expert for another expert to use as reference, but if you're expecting someone to *buy* as a result of reading the leaflet, the copy must be marketing-led (i.e. designed to promote a sale rather than to convey information). If this means compromising the technical content, you may have to consider two separate leaflets, one to impart technical information (for readers interested in maximum information) and one to stimulate a sale to less technically-minded readers.

Watch out for a writing style which falls into the trap of using clichés or jargon rather than plain English. Trying to make words sound impressive instead of focusing on clarity is an easy mistake to make. Use short words. They are easy to spell and understand. For example, compare 'use short words' with 'avoid etymological complexity'. Not only is this difficult to understand it is also irritating.

It's usually something of a challenge to get people to read your literature so don't make it harder for them than it needs to be. Your copy should be written in terms which are easily understood, and which motivate the reader with ideas and information to give them tangible benefits. Keep the copy brief and well organised, in a logical order. Not only will this help readers to grasp important details early. They are also more likely to read to the end and take action as a result.

You can find more useful information on the Plain English Commission website www.clearest.co.uk.

---

*Tip*

**Remember the overriding rules to use short words, keep copy simple, keep it clear, keep it targeted, and make sure it fulfils the need.**

---

# 11

# Production

The most important thing in planning the production of your printed literature is to avoid over-specification – or, equally dangerous, under-specification – of production requirements of the job. This is not about design or writing standards which must always reinforce all the qualities of corporate identity and visual image which by now you will have determined; it is about the technical production characteristics of the finished product.

Over-specifying means several things. You may be entranced by the wonderful visual presented by your designer for a brochure, but remember that heavyweight board covers for your four pages of text is likely to push budgets overboard. It will cost more to post. Does it really need to be gloss, or matt laminated? UV varnish to highlight selected text or photographs with a garish reflective coat is thankfully less often used now, not least because the process is not particularly environmentally friendly, but if UV varnish is suggested, question its effectiveness. Should you be using four colours when two would do? Are too many photographs indicated? Someone has to take them and they'll all need processing through film and plates for printing. Do you really need to commission an expensive illustration when a simple diagram shows all?

Conversely, under-specifying can also mean many things. Similar questions, very different answers. Do those four pages of text need bolstering by heavyweight board covers to give an air of prestige for an important launch of a new service or product for example? Would a gloss film laminated cover provide some extra polish you'd like for a ritzy presentation, or is the practicality of a matt film laminated one needed to avoid finger marks spoiling the effect of an overall solid colour on the front cover? It would be a mistake to use a lightweight, flimsy paper for a single sheet leaflet to promote something which you expect the customer to spend considerable amounts of money on. Should the brochure be using full colour rather than black on white? Would more photographs help to get over the message?

All self-evident points when you think about it, and let's be careful not get too bogged down in detail. There are far too many options to attempt listing here and I hope you get the gist of what I am saying. Make sure the specification is fit for purpose and does nothing to erode perception of the firm either way.

We're talking here about specifications benefiting *your* firm incidentally, not the designers, who invariably get more of a buzz from producing high specification full-colour work than simple one-colour work. Whether they would prefer the kudos of a good specimen brochure to show off rather than a humble leaflet is beside the point. Having said that, the right designer will always recommend the most effective specification for the job and guide you along the right track, so don't get in too much of a state about it. Just stay aware.

## Colour printing

It's worthwhile to dwell for a moment on the ramifications of those specifications should they call for full colour, by which I mean four-colour half-tone printing (as described earlier under 'jargon you'll come across'), or one or two-colour printing (called 'one-line' or 'two-line' printing in the printers' jargon).

Four-colour half-tone printing means you can include full colour photographs as well as flat colour panels made up from tints of the basic four colour inks. These are called process cyan, process yellow, process magenta and process black. This prompts a word of caution regarding reproduction of your logo. The PMS colours you specified for your corporate identity will not as a rule be matched exactly by the four-colour half-tone process. It can be very close but not exact, so it may be necessary to print your logo as an additional (fifth) PMS line colour, or restrict it to the black version. This problem will obviously not arise in black-and white (one-colour) printing jobs where you can keep the logo in black.

# Format

I'd like you first to look at format. The size A4 and its variants are undoubtedly the most universally accepted in Europe and make up the standards recognised both to comply with compatible printing systems and to meet the need of communication and business practice wherever you go.

A4 originates from within the range of international standard paper sizes known as ISO 216. A4 is a sub division of the base size of an A0 sheet having an area of one square metre. A1 is half A0, A2 half of A1 and so on down to A9. In conjunction with A sizes, there are B and C derivatives and these are used mainly for stationery items such as envelopes. A common exception to this is DL which you will find only refers to an envelope to take A4 with two horizontal folds. C6 is an envelope accommodating A4 folded twice in half (allowing a bit of space around the folded sheet – i.e. slightly larger than A6). If this is all getting a bit complicated, simply select what you need from actual examples your designer will no doubt recommend.

Interestingly ISO is not acknowledged in every country. Notably North America and Japan have their own standards, some of which use metric dimensions to fit in with ISO. Standard North American letter and envelope sizes are different from our own (hence their standard 'Letter' document size, a little longer and narrower than A4). Confusing or what, but it does explain why some of the specialist papers and boards you might see in your designer's library of samples will not comply to ISO 216. If you choose any of these to end up as an A size there is going to be cut-off waste, so as a mini tip you might be able to consider making use of those off-cuts for small items such as visiting cards or coupons and the like. Think about this in advance mind, by including them on the original print run, because it might not be possible to print them as individual pieces.

Enough of my ramblings about international paper standards. They are quite complex and I hope this sketchy outline on the subject will serve as a little background information and help you converse more comfortably with designers and printers.

One thing to remember about A sizes is that you do not *have* to use them conventionally like everybody else. This is a point often overlooked. Think about how a single sheet A4 leaflet might look if it were to be folded vertically to appear more elegant and acquire a certain element of innovation. Would that reflect well on the firm? Would it reflect even better if it was printed on thin 'snappy' card instead of paper? Then again, it could be folded to create a short front cover effect with an index or space to show a colour strip down the right hand edge linked to the open spread; or you could keep the same overall proportions and make it a three page horizontal brochure and add a narrow pocket, either glued or locked by a neat cut, at the same time.

Such ideas are not exactly new or original. It's just that people often fail to stop and think about alternatives. The key issue I am trying to highlight here is that even before we've talked about colour or graphics, there is already potential for a more interesting item of literature simply by folding a plain A4 sheet differently. This principle applies across all A sizes of course, and it is surprising how much information and visual appeal can be built in to a neat A5 leaflet folded twice horizontally. Try it!

However, I am quite prepared to concede that specifying plain and simple A4 proportions will be the most likely format on the majority of applications.

## The materials

Having decided on the format for literature, what options are there on graphics, materials and print finishes? When I said I hoped I was not going to disappoint you about exciting design because the real surprises have to come from your designer, this is the part I meant! As a graphic designer myself, I feel a certain frustration here inasmuch as by definition, graphic design is visual and here I am *writing* about it.

One way you can evaluate design proposals for your firm's literature is by taking a close look at what's been produced by others. Take time to build up a collection of brochures. Visit a few showrooms and pick up their literature; alternatively send off for it. It's usual for the big names in business to get it right (but not always the case). You'll also find that smaller specialist organisations often produce work to a very high standard, but samples from these sources can be more difficult to obtain. Collect as many samples as you can from across a broad range of businesses, not limited to your own field. Design can be subjective we know, but styles and design trends will soon become apparent and those which appeal to you will stand out a mile. I am not suggesting copying any one of them, but being well informed about what else is around is going to help enormously when it's time to make decisions on your own literature.

Here are a few combinations you might look out for.

A heavier weight board cover can add prestige to an otherwise modest four or six page leaflet using 150gsm paper. By the way, the trade always refer to 'weights' of board and paper, not thickness. A typical weight of paper for text pages as an example, might be 180gsm for a leaflet coupled with 280gsm board for the cover. The paper stock for this book, by way of comparison, is 100gsm). Always see samples and obtain comparative costs before deciding what to use.

Even if it costs more, it's often worthwhile bulking up the text page paper weights to get a better 'feel' to a catalogue. A heavier paper stock is also less liable to get torn, creased or crumpled if a long service life is anticipated.

If your brochure is more than twenty-eight pages, consider using a text page sheet as the cover (known as a 'self-cover'). You could also consider folding the front cover to double up its thickness. Self-covers *can* save you money on material, but always check out blank dummies using different weights and cover material combinations before deciding. You may have to buy board backed envelopes to compensate if literature is too flimsy and open to possible damage in the post.

Get creative with bindings. To introduce stiffness and give an air of substance, use a double crease for the spine, and staple or stitch pages into the bottom crease. This also works with spiral bindings and effectively makes for a clean front cover area by hiding the spiral on the back.

Make an imposing statement by having the covers oversize relative to inside bound text pages. This tactic however will depend on dimensions of the base sheet being used, and take care to see that it still fits your envelopes.

Recall if you will the comments regarding format. Now leave those confines of A4 behind. I'm sure you'll find the world's become your oyster!

Suddenly, publications can be square and sophisticated, long and thin, tall and elegant, thick-bound and squat. Think about fold-out pages, concertina pages, inserts, flaps, tabs and indexes. Then play more tunes with print finishes from matt or gloss laminates, embossing, metallic foil stamping, matt inks on gloss, gloss inks on matt. Combine such things with different paper and board stocks from sensual smooth and matt, to crackly bond, shiny art, textured wove, laid and embossed finishes. There's an extravaganza of soft felt boards, metallic surfaces, fluorescent colours, bright flat colours, pastel shades, speckled and deckle edged stock all waiting to be discovered. It is a never-ending list which seems to grow by the day, each category having its own sub menu of choices and variations from paper and board makers the world over.

Being aware of such a riot of alternatives is but a beginning to a very exciting and rewarding episode in creating literature that looks good, and works well to elevate perception of your firm above and ahead of the competition. You're going to have a great time discussing it all with your design team.

Whilst on the subject of elevating perception of the firm, always, always include a personally signed letter with your literature when sending it out by post in response to an enquiry. Not only is this basic rule of etiquette often forgotten, it also means passing up a valuable first opportunity to interact with the customer, let alone the means of a friendly follow up telephone call.

> *Tip*
>
> **What you look like in visual terms is just part of the story, make sure everything that's written, as well as everything that's printed, work together as champions of your identity.**

# 12

# Direct Mail

I received a direct mail shot this morning. From a charity. A veritable cacophony of elements stuffed in a non-standard window envelope printed with 'Urgent, open now' messages. Nothing to say whether or why it was worthwhile opening urgently and it could easily have been from – well, anyone really. Inside were a letter, several leaflets on assorted grades of paper bearing entirely different designs, a reply-paid envelope, a research form and an offer to respond for a gift item of dubious value. The logo appeared somewhere on each of the leaflets but was tucked away in odd corners in small sizes and seemed intended as only a token gesture in an attempt to promote recognition.

The intentions of the charity were, of course, to be applauded, but the execution of the mailshot left me exasperated and wondering why so much time and effort had gone into producing such an expensive, yet cheap-feeling mish-mash. It is to be hoped that the response will have by now justified the mailing, but if the identity had been created right first and followed through properly, much of the expense of originating different leaflet designs would have been saved. As well as preserving funds in the bank, the charity and its aims would also have benefited from being recognised and remembered more easily, thus helping to improve response both on this occasion and future appeals too. The letterhead had rather a good design and why this basis was not used for the other items remains a mystery to me.

There was also a mailshot from a German car maker in the same post. What an astounding difference. Instantly recognisable, clean design and a clear message with the simple response mechanism of a reply-paid post card already filled in with name and address details. The salutary and somewhat sad fact to observe was that this mailshot from a mega-rich corporation undoubtedly cost rather less than the one from the charity, yet its appeal and likely response levels were destined to be infinitely higher.

I think one of the lessons to be learned has to be: **'Set out what you want your mailshot to achieve and then simplify the method required to reach that objective.'**

Why use direct mail when there are other ways of communicating with your customer? Considering the cost of design and printing of the leaflet, plus a covering letter, plus a reply-paid card or envelope, plus postage, Doesn't this make direct mail very expensive in comparison to say an advertisement? You may even think of putting a leaflet as a **loose insert** in a magazine as an alternative to direct mail. Indeed this is an alternative which should not be discounted – response rates are typically much lower, but you're looking an insertion charge of perhaps one third of the cost of posting your leaflet direct, and much lower production costs (no envelopes, no covering letter, and no envelope-stuffing!). The obvious trouble with this route is that your stuff can get swamped by everyone else's loose inserts, and many magazine readers shake out all the inserts into the waste-paper bin without even looking at them!

I think the primary advantage of direct mail is that you can be fairly confident, assuming of course that both your targeting and data base is good, that when the prospect receives post either at home or at work your message will be picked up, opened and read. If you've done it right and get lucky, you'll get a response. At the very least you'll create presence for your firm right there in their hand.

Anything arriving on someone's desk or dropping through their letterbox is generally looked on as being personal for them, and first impressions of politeness and good business practice are important. You want your firm to be regarded in the correct light right from the beginning. If it's your first contact with a new customer it may be the start of something big, and if it's someone already buying from you, you need to keep in their good books!

When you decide to post personally addressed mail, make sure you use open and close your letter accordingly. For example, don't address the envelope to Mr S. Gibson, and then begin the letter 'Dear Sir or Madam', and don't forget to sign off the letter with a signature of the person who will handle the response.

Alternatively you could mail out without any name or individual address and send to specific postcodes. A variation of this is door-to-door leaflet drops by local newspapers or specialised distribution contractors who bundle in your mailing with others. Here again the problem of being swamped out raises it's unwelcome head.

The database you use is crucial. Verify that it is up bang to date, because it is possible for a list to decay by up to 40% over a year. People move or die, companies move or go out of business, and even the original list can be incorrect or incomplete. So watch out.

At this juncture I would like to drop in a reminder that the purpose of this book is not to offer technical advice on the specific nuances and techniques of direct mail, or of any other promotional activity for that matter, but to focus on the way that such activities influence perception of your firm. This begs the question: 'OK then, how *does* direct mail influence perception of my firm?'

You'll probably guess by now what I am about to say. Whatever mailshot you originate, make sure it's designed to be part of the plan and a recognised element of your corporate identity programme. Having said that, also make sure that your mailshot is seen appropriately when it reaches its destination. It's out there fighting for the firm all alone so make the package or envelope stand out from general mêlée of junk mail. Colour, size and texture come to mind. Yours won't be junk after all. When opened, its contents have to keep alive the promises of that package and relegate other stuff in the mail to at least second place for attention.

The series of direct mail packs illustrated on page 94 was sent over a period of about six weeks, and was aimed at prospective customers who were mainly unaware of the wide range of the benefits offered by the company. Each one makes it easy and convenient for recipients to respond by including a reply paid card attached to the leaflets, an explanatory letter with contact details, and a reference to all the other products available. Information received from completed reply cards can be used to build a data base, but don't forget restrictions of the data protection legislation.

*Sample direct mail pack*

Direct mail is used by all types of businesses, in all sectors, because it is a targeted and highly personal form of marketing enabling you to know exactly to whom you are talking. It follows from this that your identity will be playing a front line role and I believe it is very important not to let the underlying purpose of the mailing undermine it. Sure, you have to maximise response by highlighting benefits and telling the reader what you have for sale, that goes without saying. You may want graphics that shout and scream out the message, but don't become so preoccupied that you forget about the rules of your visual image.

Whether you are promoting an amazing offer, introducing a new product range, sending information about an exciting technical development, or making a broad selling pitch for prospective new customers, make sure beyond doubt that the message is seen and identified as coming from *your* firm.

> *Tip*
>
> **Focus on the target, check the data base is accurate and up to date, and preserve the principles of your visual identity.**

# 13

# Public Relations

In its broadest sense, Public Relations covers every aspect of your communication with the public at large, including not only press releases, corporate brochures, reports and accounts, but every type of promotional activity which involves the production of printed material. Naturally all this material will bear visual evidence of your identity.

But what of the non-visual aspects of PR – the nurturing of reputation? As I said at the very beginning, what you look like in visual terms is just part of the story. Like it or not, you'll have a reputation to develop and protect, too. It's not an option. What you do, what you say and what others say about you, word of mouth if you like, is building a reputation of some kind and creating a perception of the firm quite distinct from its visual one.

Public Relations is an additional way to build and care for your reputation across all of those groups we identified when answering the question of who looks at your firm. PR is not just what you write and publish; it is how you behave –  the glue which holds it all together. It can have a big influence on how the business is perceived and provides the means for a small company to think big, and even on a minimal budget, look it as well.  It's a fact of life that a small supplier gets treated differently to a large supplier.

A popular misconception is to regard PR as primarily concerned with 'spin' and to think of media such as newspapers, radio and television as being the only channels for its employment. Nothing is further from the truth and whilst I admit that media is the engine room of PR, you must understand its wider aims of earning support and influencing behaviour together with its ability to shift opinion to achieve a competitive advantage. It's more about making sure your public know how and why your firm is different.

When the time comes to taking a role in paving the way to opening new markets, and even fighting your corner in times of crisis, you'll be glad of the reputation PR has projected, protected and enhanced for you.

Bill Gates of Microsoft is reputed to have once said: 'If I was down to my last dollar, I'd spend it on PR.'

As Gates realised all to well, good PR is as important for big firms as it is for small ones.

Can you do PR yourself? It's essential that you do. At every opportunity, and that probably means several dozen times a day when you're talking to customers, suppliers, staff, and public and so on. When you start to organise events and presentations, involve the media, or wish to influence people and situations in the ways we've just been looking at it might be wise to consider hiring a professional. On the whole, journalists are very busy, deadline-driven people. If you have someone 'in the know' and regarded as an independent corroborator of your story you stand a better chance of being heard. It can make life much easier for the journalist to action a story if it is recognised as coming from a dependable source.

You can search for a PR professional in much the same way as described in finding a designer except that there are only two main categories you need to consider.

The first of these is an independent or freelance consultant. You will not, I imagine, be giving one person enough work to keep them occupied full time. Undoubtedly they will be engaged on a number of separate projects for different clients at the same time as yours, and you'll need to know if they are flexible and able to offer both interim and long-term support. They may have assistants or other staff to help out on administration, but don't be too distressed if the main guy is unavailable, because PR is a business where everyone usually gets stuck in to give client's the five star service they expect. Your account will be valuable to an individual or a smaller organisation. You know that from your own experience.

The second choice you have is to use a Consultancy. These vary greatly in size, from the large City-based consultancies with international offices around the world, to small locally-based independent firms.

As referred to above, choosing a PR consultant is much like choosing a design consultant; choose one who appears to understand your business, who has proven and relevant expertise in the field, who seems to be good at coming up with new ideas, and who fits within your budget. If you are going for one of the larger firms, don't be put off by grand or expensive-looking offices, as such consultancies often have lower profile satellite units which handle less affluent clients who may still need occasional access to a network of well connected high-fliers.

For more information and help finding a PR professional, look at the Chartered Institute of Public Relations website: www.cipr.co.uk.

Whoever you choose to work with, have a detailed picture of the achievements you are aiming for. Be prepared for questions on your thinking because the onus will be on them to deliver, and you'll need to be told what will and what won't work. Talk to the people you will be working with and establish ground rules of sharing values of openness and trust. PR runs very close, inseparable even, to the very soul of your business. Your survival depends on reputation and if that's lost, it's gone forever.

---

*Tip*

**Make sure you multiply the number of opportunities to be noticed by letting Public Relations have a say in how your firm behaves and how it presents itself.**

---

# 14

# Press releases and press relations

There are many folks who get the wrong idea by thinking that press releases constitute PR. As we've seen, PR is a lot more besides. Nevertheless, there is great value in maintaining regular output of press releases, press information, media release sheets; call them what you will.

I would counsel – especially in the context of 'you can't do it all' and probably don't have the time to either – that you would be wise to seek out a PR professional willing to take on the task of writing and despatching press releases. Like most of the issues we've considered, consistency is key to success, and it's simply no good to either you or the press to endure the pain of spasmodic attempts for coverage in their publication only when you manage to get round to doing it. I've known clients who attack the prospect of creating press releases with vigour, only to find enthusiasm waning when 'news' stories dry up or they've found other more important things to do instead. One undesired repercussion is that the press also lose interest, generating inevitable negative feelings towards your firm.

Do you know what the press look for in a release? Key issues for journalists are: Is this news? Does it fit my audience and readers interests? Will it fit the space? What's the people angle? What's the business and industry angle? Does it use appropriate language?

Your communication should not only be tailored to be of interest to each different audience by speaking with them in a language they understand, but also mimic the writing style of the media you are sending it to. The local newspaper may be ecstatic about your plans to increase the number of employees, but it won't mean diddly-squat to national press.

So, writing a press release may not be as straightforward as many people think. Nationally distributed newspapers and magazines distributed nationally are extremely selective in their coverage, and are far more difficult to get into than local press. You'll have to consider timing too. No one is interested in spreading the word about a wonderful development that you forgot to tell them about last year. Find out if any features about your business sector are planned and consider if it's worth holding off release of information until then.

Your reputation rests on consistency, and if you are going to do your own press releases make sure you keep up a steady flow of well written, informative material. Get to know the editors and journalists if you can. Build a rapport where in times of a crisis happening in your field of operation, they turn to you for comment and informed views of a situation. Look upon it as another non-visual opportunity to capture awareness of your identity and promote the values the firm stands for.

## Press advertisements

These also represent an aspect of press relations. Judicious placement of advertisements in relevant press can provide a powerful reinforcement of any feature coverage you achieve through the distribution of press releases.

In any event, as I said earlier, you will undoubtedly be bombarded by publishers' representatives and telephone sales enthusiasts all willing to take your money with unprecedented bargains... You need to differentiate between opportunists and those who are genuinely working in you best interests. When you are a regular advertiser, and it matters not whether we're talking national or local press, trade journal or consumer magazine, building a friendly welcoming relationship with the people working on the publication can create a number of mutual benefits. How often are you likely to miss a deadline because of late copy and call your account manager in the newspaper's advertising department to bend the rules a little? Could you benefit from first refusal on a last-minute bargain for an outside front cover, when the rep is desperate to fill the space and the price has been slashed? (Yes, I know I said plan on your terms and not the publishers' terms but it sometimes works in your favour to take advantage of a really good deal.) What are the chances of being successful negotiating cost reductions on space or securing special positions without extra charge? Did you hear the insider gossip about one of your competitors?

You'll find when you have a good rapport such benefits are readily available and put at your disposal, so don't (as some companies do) leave the rep hanging about in the reception waiting just to write down your order.

# Newsletters

An extension of press releases and press relations is the newsletter. Here again lurks the problem of finding enthusiasm waning when 'news' stories dry up or there are other more important things to do instead. The first issue is easy, the second not so bad, the third issue might just becoming a tad tedious and by number four it may be downright exasperating! I've seen it happen many times, I regret to say.

Such well-known problems aside, a well produced and informative newsletter packed full of interesting stories can be a useful adjunct to both PR and literature programmes. Decide at the outset who will be responsible for gathering the stories and writing it. Will you need professional help? Naturally its design will follow the corporate style but you must also make a distinction on its intended readership. Are customers to be targeted or staff? Contents must never be the same for both audiences. If you feel there is value in keeping staff informed of the company's progress, its plans for the future and so on, as a small enterprise it might not be worth the expense of a hefty full colour production. It will be more important in any event to maintain an appearance of the newsletter at regular intervals. The same goes for customer editions. Don't start in good faith, then stop production. It can damage your reputation and the perception that the firm knows where it's going. Receiving a newsletter should be an enjoyable experience and you'll want people to look forward to their next copy, not wonder if there's ever going to be another one.

> *Tip*
>
> Whatever routes you choose to follow, it will help your firms reputation and its identity to build a solid working relationship with the press in all its guises from editorial to advertising sales.

# 15

# Websites

Do they work? This question applies both to the basic mechanics of the website, and also to the commercial benefits it offers to the organisation.

The earlier section on choosing your website designer outlines some of the technical issues you need to watch out for to ensure such issues of practicality are met. However, whilst those are highly relevant points to remember there is an obvious question to ask. Do you need a website in the first place? And what do you want it to achieve for you?

Current widespread advice is that every company *must* have a website to even have a hope of surviving in today's ultra competitive trading conditions, but before you leap in consider if a website is pertinent to your business and are likely customers ever going to visit it? For most businesses, the answer is undoubtedly yes – but only if it is properly designed, and integrated and incorporated in all of you corporate communications. However, for some businesses the benefits of having a website may not be so clear.

A guy approached me one day with an innovative idea about a new kind of fast food snack, ideally suited for selling at outdoor shows, sporting events and so on. He seemed desperate to have a website created, but when we looked at the offering more closely it became apparent that it was highly unlikely anyone would be prompted by information gleaned off the internet to search out and buy the product. Even if anyone bothered to look for it. By its very nature, this was destined to be an initial impulse purchase which would only be followed by repeat buying if the consumer felt satisfied and discovered the stall at another outdoor event. This was the way the snack would build a reputation for quality and increase sales over time. A website would therefore be redundant, and the somewhat limited promotional budget would work better if it were directed towards other areas, notably point of sale and presentation.

However, there is a twist to this tale. In our initial discussion he failed to mention plans were under way to build a franchise network. This totally altered the circumstances of promoting his product and the idea of a website suddenly became feasible again.

The need for a website is primarily driven by its ability to generate either sales or positive PR. For most companies, this will indeed be the case – but not for all!

Some companies go for a compromise solution, by simply have a holding page giving contact details. This can be frustrating for browsers who are looking to find out about the company, but at least it provides a further point of contact. And most importantly, it can always be developed later.

If you do follow the overwhelming trend and develop a fully operational website, it is vital that the site reflects the visual corporate identity referred to in earlier sections.

Finally, two words of advice for the DIY website developer:

1.  Help buyers to find whatever you're selling by an efficient navigation system within a logical structure. If it's easy for site visitors to find what they are looking for, the more likely they are to buy; and when this is presented in the framework of a visual identity they recognise, it makes a sale even more probable.

2.  Make descriptions accurate and pricing clear. It can avoid all manner of after-sales problems. Remember there are obligations under the *Consumer Protection (Distance Selling) Regulations 2000* to comply with.

---

*Tip*

**Think about if you really need a website. If you do, build it properly and make sure it's working for you at every level.**

---

# 16

# Outdoor advertising

When you think about it, billboards and posters provide a great way of getting your firm and its identity noticed, especially in targeted or localised areas. I reckon the majority of outdoor advertising is more of a PR device than a sales generating activity as generally, unlike press ads and direct mail, the audience will rarely respond directly. How frequently have you sat in a traffic jam and scrabbled for a pen and paper to write down a telephone number from the poster on the back of a bus in front? Exactly.

On the other hand, everyone who gets out and about is usually exposed to outdoor advertising of one form or another, and they don't need to turn over a page, open the post, or do anything at all to be influenced by your message.

The value of 'the good idea' in outdoor advertising is arguably more pivotal for achieving recognition than in any other media. People on the move have only seconds to absorb your message, particularly when it's on a busy road or street poster site. So keep what you are saying simple, sharp and to the point, and use as few words as possible. A senior marketing man in Shell once said to me: 'Five words are just right.'

If you can get away with just one word, your name and a picture, so much the better. That is why the 'good idea' behind those few words and possibly a picture are so critical.

The jargon 'dwell time' is not as critical in locations such as railway stations or in a shopping precinct for example where readers have a little more time for contemplation. Introduce an element of humour and you encourage familiarity; a chuckle always helps to get people on your side. This doesn't alter the need for a 'good idea', mind, and – you've guessed already – the chance to reinforce perception of the firm with all the visual qualities of your corporate identity.

I've used the term 'outdoor advertising' somewhat loosely to mean any advertising or information material that is literally seen out and about. The definition covers a surprising diversity of applications. A giant ninety-six sheet poster is probably on your list for later, so here's a slightly longer one to consider in the short term. It's not exhaustive by any means but I hope it helps to outline a few possibilities for you to mull over:

- Roadside posters and High Street billboards
- Railway platforms and bus stations
- Train and bus interiors
- Bus exteriors and taxis
- Post offices and airports
- Shopping malls and leisure centres

You might even consider small posters (not the hand-written kind) displayed in local retail outlets. Don't knock it if that doesn't sound prestigious enough for you, because there are times when these things work. One of my clients who ran a couple of upmarket gastro-pubs in a tourist area enjoyed considerable success by spreading the name around the locality in places seen by visitors.

A poster is unlike leaflet. Or an advertisement. People generally do not stop and study messages on posters or have time to read detailed sales pitches. A marketing and promotions manager at Shell once told me that the shorter, and simpler the message the better. Five words are just right he said. It's a piece of good advice that has proved its worth many times over. Take a look at posters used by major advertisers and you will find that fewer words always make a more effective, and memorable message, usually quite independent of any graphics or photography. Remember these principles work just as well on small promotional placards and the like.

The number of advertisers committing funds to outdoor advertising continues to grow and is evidence of growing confidence in the medium. Is it right for your firm? It all depends! If you want to influence a mass audience as they pass by, or focus on your locality to enhance perception of what you do, outdoor advertising might be worth thinking about. There's more information at www.oaa.uk.

> *Tip*
>
> **Don't expect to get loads of direct response from poster advertising.**

# 17

# Vehicles

Closely following outdoor advertising, and very much a part of essential basic elements of your corporate identity, is the way you mark out vehicles, put your name on the outside of your premises, and display signs and directions around the site and throughout its interior. Vehicles, premises and signage are all vitally important to perceptions of the firm, but are frequently neglected in favour of a temporary, ill-advised expedient simply because someone is unsure of quite what to do.

Let's start with vehicles. Only a few manufacturers seem to construct bodywork with sign-writing in mind, and unless your identity has been designed for a specific vehicle (highly unlikely) there are panel shapes, joints, and doors in all the wrong places! Compromise has to be the order of the day, which is why it is unwise to leave it to the sign-writer to do the best he can. You and your designer are the only people who can be expected to fully understand all the ramifications of what your visual style sets out to achieve and it is certainly best practice to provide the sign-writer with accurate working drawings that properly adapt your identity to fit to the vehicle involved. I use the term 'sign-writing' advisedly, but of course you will know the current term to use should be 'vehicle livery'. I am never quite sure what to call the people who apply graphics to vehicles these days. Traditional sign-writers are very rare. Perhaps 'digitalised vinyl livery application technicians' would be appropriate because technology has given us some wonderful techniques and effects. Just about anything graphic; photos, lettering, illustrations, and logos can be put on to your vehicle at virtually any size and in any colour you decree. At a cost. You'll find a natural eagerness for 'digitalised vinyl livery application technicians' to demonstrate their prowess. I'm not knocking them in any way and let there be no misunderstanding on this point because the results can be stunning. If you're sure the firm will benefit from a full colour photographic image across the whole side of a delivery van for example, go for it. Just remember the maxim that a good idea is infinitely more valuable than any highly finished visual packaged simply to make that idea look superficially impressive. This is why you need your designer's interpretation of the design compromises which will almost certainly be required, and for accurate working drawings to be supplied.

Most manufacturers provide outline diagrams of their vehicles to permit precise specifications, and you'll most probably also be able to access these details at your 'digitalised vinyl livery application technicians'. As part of the technical specification, ask for a quote to include the option of a carrier film for the graphics. This allows the vehicle to be more easily returned to its original finish without permanent adhesive marks, thus retaining a higher residual resale value.

I found this 'Hammond' example in the archives (they used to be a small business producing poultry and eggs) and included it to prove that when you start right with a strong logo and apply it consistently you'll have an identity which lasts. This was launched early in 1960 and would still be successful as a striking image on our roads today - on a modern vehicle that is!

The MEB cherry picker (below) is one of a large fleet of many different vehicles emphasising part of the logo seen across other aspects of promotion and internal communications. It carries a very powerful image which is easily remembered because of its dynamic simplicity.

---

*Tip*

Keep vehicle livery strong, striking, legible, and resist the
temptation to include too much detail.

---

# 18

# Exterior signage

Of course, the firm's name has to be in style on the front of the building somewhere, but sometimes it's difficult to correlate the design of your corporate identity with the needs of architectural features and at the same time comply with local authority planning regulations. It is impossible to be specific here because of constraints unique to your property, so here are a few general tips to watch out for:

♦ Keep a watchful eye on the sign's condition. It is amazing how quickly the weather and sunlight can affect colour and materials to make the sign, and consequently the name of the firm, look tatty and neglected.

♦ Light and time of day make big differences to appearances so discuss this aspect before installation. For example, a back illuminated sign can look great at night, but if individual plastic panels are joined unevenly and have even a slight ripple, the sign will look particularly awful in acutely angled sunlight.

♦ Consider not having a large sign at all. Lettering and logos in cut-out form (not reproduced on white cards which give a terrible, cheap impression) can look very effective applied on glass doors for example. You might even think about a variation on the traditional brass plate by using some other material instead. Keep it clean and well polished, though! There's an optometrist in my local town who has a dull and dirty brass plate sign mounted on a faded wooden block which does nothing to promote any confidence in his abilities whatsoever. Perhaps he thinks an eye test before you enter is a good idea!

- If you have to mount direction signs, to a car park for instance, make sure you use the corporate font, or typeface, in the appropriate colour. I have a thing against standard signing systems and believe visitors should be 'wrapped in your identity' at the earliest opportunity. By the way, don't reserve car parking spaces nearest the front door for yourself or staff. It creates a better perception of thoughtfulness and respect if these are kept free for the convenience of customers.

Sometimes exterior signs on your own premises have a much more difficult job to do than simply inform, direct or warn. There is an enormous amount of competition fighting for attention, and like posters, signs have to be easily assimilated and recognised in the shortest possible time. Establishing a clear identity and keeping it consistent helps. It doesn't end there of course, as in some situations, such as the Steptoes Market example below on page 117, the signing has to ensure there's no mistaking what the business is all about even before you step across the road. In other cases, like the Brandoon Tool Hire example on page 117, standing out from the crowd can be a challenge!

---

*Tip*

**Make sure your identity and your property work together in harmony because it's not just customers you have to please.**

---

*Signage at Steptoes Market*

*Signage at Brandon Tool Hire*

# 19

# Interiors

How often, as a visitor to business premises, have you witnessed a variety of ragtag notices, usually typed on thin copy paper stuck on to walls with short lengths of crinkled sticky tape? Doctors waiting rooms seem to be a good example of this technique: they're not trying to sell anything but information would be more easily assimilated if it were better organised and presented.

We established earlier the fact that one of the principle ways to help make the most of how your business is perceived is to properly control identity across everything that's done. There is no more fragile environment than the inside of your premises. Under your very nose is the Achilles heel of untidiness and evidence of careless appearance: the typed out notice for fire drill stuck on the wall; the last delivery of half empty cardboard box's littering the reception area; the instructions for visitors to lift the telephone and dial for attention; opened magazines and remains of staff snacks at break visible on desks, and so on. These are things which let down an otherwise favourable perception of so many companies, and I include in that some multinational organisations I have worked for in the past.

The problem is that it's so easy, so very easy in the clamorous rush of everyday working, to let standards of identity slip. Inevitably with that goes a chunk of the perceptions of quality and the values you've been working so hard to establish.

It is also very easy to take control and responsibility for keeping such matters up to scratch on a regular basis. Making sure all internal signs, directions and instructions comply with your style, for instance. Reflecting the principles of a well executed identity by ensuring working areas are maintained and seen to be well ordered and tidy, for another instance. Then you could take the opportunity of using space in reception to have a show-case of literature, products and packaging along with some really good photographs to demonstrate manufacturing processes or to show your people at work. Don't ever let that space become cluttered by anything else. Make your visitors feel comfortable by providing seating which doesn't look like a cast-off from the Ark or a mismatch of old chairs from around the office. Or worse. Is the decoration clean and fresh? Quite apart from any special paint jobs in corporate colours, do not expect scuffed and grubby magnolia emulsion to fire up people's enthusiasm for the firm.

Are these things important? Do they matter and will it make any difference? An elderly aunt of mine maintained that if you want to find out what someone is really like, you need to follow them home. I reckon that's a good dictum for business too. If visitors are given an experience which highlights your other activities and what they've seen of you elsewhere it can only enhance their perception of your firm as being the one to do business with, or worthwhile carrying on doing business with – and that can't be bad. You may even be setting them an example of how to do things more effectively, and that can't be bad, either!

---

*Tip*

**Interior manifestations of your corporate identity at home should look as good and work as well as those seen out and about in the big wide world.**

---

# 20

# Exhibitions and shows

If you want to set up a successful stand at an exhibition or show, there's one big secret to share with you: Time. That's Time with a capital T by the way, because you are going to need to spend more of it than you think. Time to plan. Time to prepare. Time to take care of all those little details that are going to happen on the day of opening. There is no room to manoeuvre on the date the exhibition opens.

Invariably a commitment to attend a show is made months before the event and preparations get put on the back-burner because 'there's plenty of time'. Well, there isn't! Deadlines have a habit of unobtrusively creeping up on you. For a start you'll have to fill out various forms on different dates specified in the organiser's manual for exhibitors to meet deadlines running up to the opening day. You'll need to decide what electric supplies and on-stand catering arrangements you'll need. Not to mention putting together the promotional material, preparing exhibits, support advertising, invitations and briefing staff, plus maybe arranging their accommodation. These are only a few of the things. There's a lot more to think about, lots to do, and the sooner you begin to plan and take action the better.

If you think I'm making too much of a thing about time, I write having had direct experience seeing senior executives of big-name companies flung into a state of last-minute panic and confusion simply due to their failure to put plan ahead for the deadlines. I have witnessed instances on neighbouring stands where personnel have been absent after the exhibition has opened, leaving customers to gaze vacantly around a deserted stand. You can imagine what that does for perceptions of their company.

There are many categories of exhibitions which might interest you, ranging from vast indoor venues featuring international exhibitors to county shows in tents. The principles of design and presentation are much the same for all of them. You either buy floorspace where you are totally responsible for construction of the stand, or you buy a shell scheme where, subject to individual organisers' rules, you are given a booth which already has walls, ceiling and basic lighting and electric outlets provided. You can usually add to the basic specification, and upgrade power supply, furniture, lighting, etc. (Upgrading lighting can be particularly worthwhile.) The shell scheme route is generally much the cheaper option, but offers much less scope to stand out from the crowd..

Where you are buying floorspace rather than a shell scheme, you will need an exhibition designer and contractor to do all the construction and installation. It is essential that you thoroughly brief them on the principles of your corporate identity, and that you take the time to plan and work alongside them at every stage. With the right brief, and careful monitoring along the way, all should be well and you can arrive on opening day with a relaxed flourish!

In the case of a shell scheme there are rather more options to consider, the main one being are you going to do it all yourself or employ an element of stand designer's or contractor's help?

Let's start at the bottom and work up, and you can decide how much help you might need. The disadvantage of any shell scheme is that you can end up looking like everyone else, but this is not an insurmountable problem. There are several ways to make your firm stand out without it costing the earth.

There will be a fascia board with your company name on it in the same typeface as all the other shell stands and there is nothing you can do about this. Make a difference by getting your name and logo big and legible on all walls of the shell. Remember delegates will be approaching from both ends of the aisle if your stand is in a row with others. If you are on a corner site it is easier to be noticed.

Most exhibitors will be hiring furniture from the organiser's designated suppliers so make a difference and take your own. Do not, however, under any circumstances, take a trestle table or the like and cover it with a cloth. You'll probably see someone doing just that and I'll leave you to draw your own conclusions about what sort of firm it looks like in comparison to others. You can find furniture hire companies which will provide alternative designs independently of the organiser's suppliers.

Most exhibitors will use the shell lighting. This is usually minimal, so make a sparkling difference by arranging for extra lights.

Most exhibitors will hang very rough and ready pictures, diagrams or graphic panels on the shell walls (which more often than not are in a weedy pastel colour). You can make an impressive difference by 'dry lining' the stand with your own graphics.

Most exhibitors will make do with only the basic pastel coloured walls of the shell, and then litter what space remains visible with boxes of sales brochures, coats and briefcases and the like. You can make a big difference by building in a cupboard or screened area which can be used to not only show off your identity to good effect, but also hide impedimenta and make space for preparing drinks or refreshments for visitors.

By way of example, the Energy Services exhibition stand (see below) makes the most of a relatively small floor area. Notice the strong presence of the logo easily visible from whichever direction a visitor approaches. Good lighting 'springs' it out, and reflects the clinical nature of its industrial style structure. There are places to sit for discussion, a promotion to draw visitors on to the stand, and no untidy clutter to impair corporate identity.

*Energy Services' Exhibition Stand*

Small businesses often take advantage of using a shell scheme (as referred to above) rather than run to the expense of buying floor space only and building a stand from scratch. Shell schemes have their limitations however, particularly when one needs to make a statement on identity. There are some tips to help get around these restrictions and make your stand stand out as it were. You cannot do anything about the company name on the fascia as this is fixed by the organisers of the exhibition, so it helps to ensure your logo is instantly visible from the aisle. Make sure you use plenty of lights. This alone can make you sparkle in front of your neighbours. Take a corner site if you can and you will steal another visibility advantage. Keep the stand scrupulously clean and tidy at all times. A promotion such as a daily draw will encourage more visitors on to the stand rather than letting them stroll past.

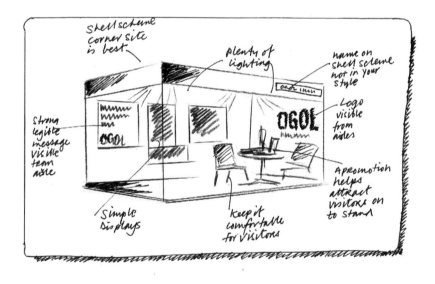

*Sample 'shell scheme' exhibition stand*

Nothing to do with graphics but a lot to do with perceptions of the firm is attitude, and how people staffing the stand dress and behave. Much hard work and time goes into putting an exhibition stand together, not to mention money. It all gets blown in two or three days more or less, so maximise every moment available. Everybody involved should be made fully aware that in no way is it an excuse for a jolly. It can be tedious, tiring work. It is also one of the few situations in business when you are seen literally next-door to your competitors, so everyone on the stand has to be bright and on the ball always. Seating is for visitors not staff; at break times go somewhere else.

Neither is an exhibition an alternative to 'proper' sales activity. You may have the sneaking suspicion that while you are away the firm's daily needs are being neglected in some way. This comment is prompted by opinions I've heard expressed on numerous occasions, mainly by field sales representatives who would rather be 'out there' rather than stuck in one stuffy place waiting for customers to walk into the stand. Indeed, I remember once visiting a client's exhibition stand in the afternoon of the day of opening and being struck dumb by the disposition of the sales manager. This tall elegant gent, whom I had met on many occasions, sat on the edge of the stand, head in hands. 'Hello, George' I said. 'How's it going?' He looked up at me with a weak smile and said: 'Hello, Sid. I hate bloody exhibitions. Waste of time. I ought to be in Sheffield now. They're not happy with me being here, y'know.'

It turned out that in Sheffield was a major customer, but unfortunately George was unaware that their MD was actually walking round the exhibition hall as he spoke.

It follows from this that you should make every effort to let customers know where you are exhibiting and send an invitation for them to visit your stand. And naturally, after the event you'll be thanking them, following up enquiries promptly and taking steps to publicise your success at the show through PR, won't you?

These are just a few of the tactics you can exploit to enhance the perceptions of your firm over the competition, and indeed quite a few of your fellow exhibitors too. In most cases, whilst I would recommend professional help from people who are in the exhibition business and understand its many nuances. To reiterate, it's how you *approach and manage* these issues which are important.

> *Tip*
>
> **Remember that exhibitions will take up more of your time than you think.**

# 21

# TV and local radio

Are they worth the money?

I'm going to dispense with the notion of TV advertising right away. As touched upon earlier, whenever advertising is discussed socially you'll find it's generally television advertising in the firing line and rarely newspaper or magazine advertising, let alone the broader aspects of advertising and promotion. But I don't think television advertising is applicable here. It is without doubt a powerful medium, and if it's appropriate to what your firm does you'll most likely not be in the small business category and will have appointed an advertising agency to work for you. You cannot possibly think about doing it yourself. The high costs of production and complexities of time slots and broadcast rate structures means your commercial has to be right first time, properly targeted, properly scheduled. So that's that.

Local radio, though, may be a more relevant consideration, particularly when you have to reach the local community, either to maintain a presence or to draw attention to a promotion or event. It is manifestly impossible to back up any visual element of your corporate identity on radio, so your reputation hangs not just on what you say, but how you say it. It's back to consistent style again. And we have an additional problem inasmuch as it is all very well trying to maintain the copy-writing style you've elected to use in literature and advertisements, but with constraints of broadcast time the message must be punched home quickly.

The question remains. Is radio right for you? Let's take a look at what it offers in very broad terms.

Perhaps the biggest drawback is that your commercial won't stay around for long. This means that for maximum effect the ad must be repeated frequently to be absorbed. On the other hand a properly timed commercial can reach listeners at key points in their day and the message made relevant to what they are doing right then.

It's true to say that when someone is listening to a radio programme they are unlikely to switch off to avoid commercials, so they hear it in any event. It is also true to say that radio is a good way to reinforce and remind prospects about your messages which they may have seen in other media. So it helps to build recognition of your firm's name and what you do, if not what you look like.

We all know listening to radio is a voluntary thing, often for information and usually for relaxation. These contexts are both good for advertisers to be associated with as long as the content of both the commercial and the programme in which it is heard is relevant to listeners' needs.

Radio advertising does not need to be expensive, and can complement your other promotional activities and can be repeated with sufficient frequency to motivate the listener to take action.

## Cost of radio advertising

So how much does it cost to advertise on local radio?

Like so many things in this business, it all depends. Literally, it can vary from a few hundred to many thousands of pounds. And let's not forget recording costs either – as a challenge you might even be tempted to do a voice-over yourself and save a few bob, but can you take the risk of sounding amateurish, not to mention the hazard of unwanted sound effects?

Begin by deciding how big an area you want to cover. Is using more than one radio station going to be necessary? When are the people you want to advertise to going to be listening? Rates change according to time of day and there is no need to waste money broadcasting your advertisement simply to get an apparently good deal which includes a lot of spots at the wrong time. How big or how popular is the station? Is the radio station salesperson desperate to hit their sales target?

Your selected radio stations will probably work out their charges at a rate per thousand listeners at any one time. If, for example, their breakfast show has 200,000 listeners, buying a spot on that will cost you more than the late night show's 20,000 listeners. But don't forget – whatever time slot you choose, it's better to get your name recognised by a relevant smaller audience interested in what you're selling than a huge audience which is never likely to have the need to recall it. Having said that, your radio commercial will be more effective if you hit your definition of prospective customers as often as you can.

20,000 people hearing your ad six times might be better than those 200,000 people hearing it only twice. Obviously people are most likely to remember your name and react to what you are offering if it is repeated often. Make sure you make it as easy as possible to note down your contact details by leaving listeners enough time at the end of the commercial.

This may sound complicated, and audience targeting is indeed full of pitfalls if you have no experience of buying time. However the radio station will usually be pleased to work with you and suggest a schedule to fit your budget together with an estimated 'opportunities to hear' figure (OTH). This listening figure should use data from Radio Joint Audience Research (RAJAR) the official body owned jointly by the BBC and the Radio Centre in charge of measuring UK radio audiences. See www.rajar.co.uk.

The actual cost of a campaign will obviously depend on the length of the slot, the number of slots booked, the timing of the slots, and the number of listeners – and, of course, the production cost. Some radio stations publish "ratecard" advertising prices – most don't, and you will have to ring them to get a price. However, in all cases the costs are highly negotiable.

For an effective radio advertising campaign, you need to run the ad for a minimum of two weeks, using three or four 20 second slots per day. In a small station this may cost £500-1,000 per week, and you should repeat the sequence every four weeks. Rates for extended campaigns are much lower; for example, for a 12-month campaign in a radio station with 40,000 listeners you might expect to pay £10-15,000 for the full year. These have to be ballpark figures for rough guidance only, and it is only by talking to the stations of your choice will you arrive at the right solution within your budget. You will find staff at radio stations very helpful in his respect, so don't feel self conscious if you're not sure of the ropes!

For production purposes allow a minimum of £500 to produce a simple 30-second commercial to be broadcast from a small local station – this will cover a simple bit of scriptwriting and professional studio production. For a larger campaign, it is worth considering investing in a more elaborate "creative" (maybe an additional £500), with a customised jingle (maybe £500), and actors to voice the ads (perhaps another £1,000) – total production cost around £2,500. If you want go all out and license a famous song, add another £20-25,000!

For further information, take a look at www.rab.co.uk for information and case studies on using local radio.

> ### Tip
>
> Radio can be heard by everyone. How many listeners will really be interested in what your firm does? Check for possible wastage and use radio to complement your other activities.

# 22

# E-mail marketing and SMS

These may be new and exciting ways to reach people who might want to buy from you but there is a word of warning to heed.

Email marketing can be a very powerful tool, particularly when it is linked to a strong website. The use of email newsletters can be particularly productive. However, be aware that unsolicited e-mail, or 'spam', can be intrusive and irritating. Are you sure your customer wants to receive it and will it uphold the values of your corporate identity? For this kind of marketing to work you must ensure that recipients will generally be willing to receive and read your emails; in the case of email newsletters there should be an opt-out option to enable recipients have themselves removed from the distribution list. And, of course, the wording, graphics, and style of all email correspondence should be consistent with your house style and corporate identity as referred to in previous chapters.

The whole area of e-commerce is becoming increasingly complex, with rapidly changing technologies and a raft of consumer protection legislation which you should be sure to follow.

The rapid development of SMS marketing (marketing via mobile telephone text messages) deserves special mention. By its very nature SMS involves short messages, usually text-based (though images and website links can also be included). This presents obvious challenges, in terms of conveying a coherent and attractive message in 160 characters or less. Since recipients can find themselves charged for receiving your messages, it is essential that they have volunteered to receive SMS marketing emails ('opted in' in official terminology), and that they can just as easily opt out from receiving further emails. Use this marketing device with extreme case, unless you wish to risk undoing all the good work you have achieved by following the principles outlined in the rest of this book...

> *Tip*
>
> **E-mail marketing and SMS is powerful and personal. Make sure it's what your customers want to see from you.**

# 23

# How to make your firm look bigger and walk the walk

Small is beautiful they say, but in business terms looking insignificant can sometimes be a serious handicap. When you are very small, it could be an astute decision to create an impression that the company is bigger than it is. I am not for a moment suggesting you mislead people by telling them you have resources you haven't got, or make promises you are unable to keep, but no customer wants to deal with something that appears to be an under-resourced or half-baked operation, or use someone who looks like they're barely able to get it together. They want to feel confident.

By the same token *you* must feel confident about performing like a big company. Or does the thought of confronting big competition head to head make you nervous?

If it does, look at it this way. The only advantage large competitors have over you is most likely to be a more expansive sales and marketing organisation. Staffed by people lacking your commitment and drive most probably. But even if they have inferior products or their service falls short of yours, the bigger feel and presence of these competitors in the marketplace can persuade customers that they are better than you.

However, take away their size and what have they got left that you aren't already offering the customer, and then some?  Make sure your customers become aware of this and recognise your values. Then you won't feel nervous at all!

Conversely, it has to be acknowledged that it's worth remembering size is not necessarily a hindrance if, for instance, a small business depends on selling a highly personalised, or bespoke service. It's also true to say that sometimes smallness can be a positive advantage, for example in the field of consultancy or support services where clients in big companies can be persuaded that the smaller business is more nimble and talented.

Whatever your aspirations you must decide, but in my opinion fixing the right perception in the customer's mind that you are someone worthwhile doing business with is one of the most critical factors which will help achieve success. Or result in failure if not done properly.

Careful implementation of the techniques covered in this book will certainly help to raise your profile, and enable you to be perceived on an equal footing with other recognised companies who may have much larger marketing budgets.

In addition, technology is on your side to help pull off many master strokes of believable credibility to complement the visual aspects of looking good. If for example you use automated telephone-answering, do use not the standard voice-over message, but take the time to record your own; link enquiries direct to your mobile; ensure you have a responsive website, and set yourself up to be able to access it when you are on the move to maximise the many features of e-mail. Technology means you can have a simple desk space at home for an office and no one would know.

No matter what covert compromises you have to make, to be successful you must make your firm *look* successful from the outset. It may mean you will be called upon to play a variety of roles, even that of an illusionist! However, no matter how brilliant your smoke and mirror act, it will not work unless you are delivering the goods.

I will repeat that: *no matter how brilliant your smoke and mirror act, it will not work unless you are delivering the goods.*

Let's have a look at twenty-five ideas to make your firm look bigger. A number of these will be obvious but it's good to keep a check list of what many seasoned professionals will recognise as some of the oldest tricks in the book. I challenge you to add a few more.

1.  Ensure you've followed all the rules in this book for creating a visual identity.

2.  Always be available. If this means employing an answering service to handle incoming telephone calls then do it. It doesn't have to be an agency as long as the person managing it knows where you are and is capable of responding properly.

3. Always be responsive. It will do your reputation no good at all for customers to be kept waiting for the promised quote, letter, advice or returned telephone call.

4. Always do what you say you will do. It's surprising how many people forget what they have said, or assume because the customer has not chased them up that something is no longer important. Follow everything through to the letter - not always easy when you are very busy.

5. Pursue every enquiry until you are absolutely certain there's never going to be a sale. Good intentions and assurances from customers can frequently be obstructed by other commitments or unforeseen circumstances beyond their control. Make sure you're not forgotten in the mêlée of their own corporation's complications. You won't be regarded as a nuisance if you are sensitive and sympathetic.

6. Be punctual. This applies to everything, not just turning up on time, but also anything you told them you'd do, or send, or deliver.

7. Always aim to meet the promised delivery date but communicate if you encounter problems which may mean delays are likely. The last thing you should do is put your head in the hand hoping your customer won't notice. They will.

8. Be sympathetic to the dress code of your customers - or at least turn up looking smart.

9. Park round the back out of sight if you car's an old banger.

10. Speak using the 'we' (i.e. the firm) vernacular rather than 'I'. It makes you sound like a big company talking.

11. Always adopt a 'we can do' attitude, even if you need to call in resources.

12. Don't ever say you can and then let someone down. Reputations are instantly ruined like this.

13. Always motivate your assistants or employees, and make sure they understand where you're coming from. Train everyone to know how they

should be addressing customers and that they grasp the subtleties of your ethos and rationale.

14. Consider employing staff on a freelance basis to deal with specific circumstances, but be careful for them to work to the same high standards as everyone else on the firm.

15. Be enthusiastic and add ideas to what the customer asks for. You've been there already and have unique experience to help. Experience your customer doesn't have.

16. Build on your experience. Don't be shy about successes and who the firm has worked for, especially if there is any collaboration or connections with well known and respected names concealed on your customer listings.

17. Do your homework on the customer and you'll build a working relationship more quickly. It is always appreciated if you can demonstrate the fact that you already know something about a customer's business, how they operate and the standards they demand.

18. Make sure you're dealing at a high enough level. Don't waste time with pen pushers but remember their comments and regard for you can often influence decisions by the top man.

19. Maintain an entrepreneurial attitude. People can be motivated favourably by someone who knows where they are going and may even look upon you as a role model.

20. Negotiate with an air of authority, and I don't mean pompous. You want to set up a good deal that is good for your firm in every sense of the word. Not because you are small and therefore expected to be cheap.

21. Look after the details. They can let you down big time if you don't.

22. Make sure your presentation or sales pitch is good – really good! Rehearse, then rehearse again, in plenty of time for the 'big shot'.

23. Consider a post office box with a prestigious address (however, you can easily get found out on this one and it all falls apart when a customer wants to visit).

24. Be honest and straightforward with accurate answers to questions. If you don't know an answer don't fluff – say you'll get back to them on it.

25. Share your knowledge and experience, but don't give away secrets. It helps to build confidence when you show customers how something should be done.

Follow this advice, and combine it with a carefully controlled visual identity, and your firm *really will* look bigger than it is – and will grow as a consequence.

---

*Tip*

**Think like a big company, act like a big company and nobody will ever need to know differently.**

---

# 24

# Conclusion

You've arrived at the sharp end armed with a smartly designed logo and a brilliant corporate identity. The grand plan for implementing advertising, PR and promotions is already under way. You're looking good. The message is getting through to customers.

What's next?

There are many other facets in the network of communication and business activities which bring their own influences to bear on corporate identity and how your firm will be perceived:

- **Marketing** – where you'll be defining what customers expect and subsequently organising the firm's resources to meet those expectations. (see www.cim.co.uk).

- **Sales Management** – where customer relationships are built and processes established to link contract, stock, and production smoothly together. (see www.ismm.co.uk).

- **Market Research** – to deliver impartial information and which can also to put you in touch with both positive and negative perceptions of the firm. (see www.mrs.org.uk).

- **Benchmarking** – where your performance (and of course how you look) can be measured and compared with the best in the business. They may even use *you* as their benchmark!

- **Internet Marketing** – which rolls out your identity worldwide.

- **Telephone and Call Centre selling** – where how people are spoken to reflects directly on what customer's think of the firm.

Then there are such matters as punctual deliveries; reliable promises; value for money; complaint handling; efficient paperwork and enquiry response. It doesn't end there, of course. The more this list goes on, the more it serves very well to underline the reasons to convince you why it's important to make the most of how your firm is perceived at every opportunity and that you can achieve success by thinking in advance and properly controlling your identity across everything you do.

You encourage significant additional elements of control when you inspire all the people who work for the firm to be on your side. Staff and employees at every level occupy unique positions and are able to influence perceptions of the firm across everything they do too. Does everyone know where you are coming from and do they truly understand and support what's being done? Attitudes are crucial, and it's important for them to have training and information about what expected of them.

It helps enormously to have a corporate identity manual, or at least a printed style sheet where specifications and rules are clearly laid out for everyone's reference. Not only will this help consistency of style for items in daily use. It will also serve as a reminder of where you started. Believe me, it's very easy to forget!

Your designer will be able to advise further, but as a start here is a check list of some the details you may like to include:

- Logo (symbol, badge, crest, icon, emblem, motif) reproduced in colour and in black. Make a note of how this must appear, the surrounding space it needs, minimum size.

- The typefaces, or fonts and show examples in use.

- Layouts for every item of stationery showing the 'grid' for position of text and the required margins. This is also a good time to include instructions on how letters should be laid out and signed off. Indicate how the typing must be done. For example is the firm's name always to be in capital letters, or upper and lower case? Should it be spelled in full, or is it permissible to use 'Ltd' instead of 'Limited' for instance?

- The corporate colours together with notes on how these might vary on different applications.

- The paper specifications for stationery, and directions on labelling and packaging.

- Rules for signage, vehicle livery and technical specifications, paint references.

- Examples of acceptable styles for advertisements and other promotional material. In my experience recruitment ads seem to fall by the wayside most often because they are placed in a hurry by someone not knowing about, or forgetting the rules.

- A reference point for advice and guidance on consistency. This could either be you or your relevant professional source. I would always recommend nominated staff getting to know personnel at designers, printers, PR agency and media representatives and so on. It really does help team spirit and support for getting everything connected with identity and presentation right.

---

*Tip*

**Keep in mind that arriving at the sharp end is only the beginning.**

---

# Finally

Writing this book has in many ways become a personal reflection of the kicks I get working in design and advertising. These kicks come from several directions for different reasons, if you get my meaning, but it's always a challenge and fun to be in. If you find my book a useful guide and have fun with the challenge of everything you have to watch out for when building *your* firm's corporate identity, promoting its values and what you have to sell, then it will have fulfilled its objective.

Remember that you need to care for your identity, cherish it and make it attractive from every angle and make customers fall in love with your firm.

Finally, let me leave you with the following simple but all-important mnemonic:

**Keep It Simple: Keep It Sharp: Keep It Special:**
**and crucially, Keep In Style.**

**KIS:KIS:KIS:KIS**

# Glossary of terms

You will come across many terms and slang descriptions used in design, printing and publishing. With constant developments in technology they seem to invent something new to say every week!

This list is certainly not definitive or exhaustive, but many of the everyday terms are listed and will give you a certain voice of authority when discussing the pros and cons of the project in hand.

## Agency Commission

The revenue given to recognised agencies, i.e. those advertising agencies which have satisfied the requirements of the media proprietors for advertisements placed on behalf of a client. However, note that many small local publishers will give equivalent discounts to regular advertisers who buy space direct from them.

## Artwork or origination

This is the approved design for the advertisement, brochure, leaflet etc, developed and prepared for printing and publication with all components – logos, borders, illustrations, photographs and typeset copy – in place. It is provided on disc in digital form rather than as a flat piece of artwork.

## Broadsheet

Newspaper or magazines that are usually around A2 size, for example The Daily Telegraph.

## Bleed

When the printed image runs to the edge of an advertisement, or off the edge of a brochure.

## Circulation

The number of copies that the media sells or issues each time it is printed.

## Classified

This is the section of the media dedicated to selling products/services/jobs etc. It is made up totally of text, or 'lineage' A variation of this is 'display classified' where larger advertisements possibly also with illustrations are positioned.

## Column Width

Newspapers split pages into columns that vary in number and size. Advertisement sizes always adhere to those widths which in turn are sold by depth in centimetres. Therefore a 'single column centimetre' or 's.c.c' is the method in which ads are measured and costs quoted, For example an advertisement referred to as a '10 across 2' will measure 10 centimetres deep x 2 columns wide. Costs are quoted as s.c.c rates. However, just to confuse you space is also sold as full, half or quarter pages.

## Colour Separations

All printing in colour needs to have separations made to be able to print. Unless being printed digitally, an individual printing plate is then made from the film separations for each colour used. When colour photographs need to be reproduced, separations are made using the four-colour half-tone process.

## Copy deadline

The day and sometimes even the time of day, set by the media by which all origination must be at their premises.

## Free-sheet

Publication distributed free of charge, typically a newspaper

## Display advertisement

These can be positioned virtually anywhere within the publication.

## DPS

Double page spread where the advertisement runs over two pages.

## Earpiece

The small advertisements positioned alongside the 'masthead' or name of the newspaper. Earpieces can also be on the back page.

## GSM
Grammes per square meter used as a measurement for weight of paper, i.e. a square meter of 90 gsm paper would weigh 90 grammes.

## ISO
Standard international paper sizes. See "Stock"

## Lamination
Used to finish printed material with film, usually on the covers. Lamination can be flat matt or gloss.

## Media
The generic term for any carrier of a message – newspapers, magazines, radio, TV, billboards, and publications etc.

## OBC, IBC and IFC
Outside back cover, inside back cover and inside front cover.

## Paper set advertisements
Ads prepared by the media for the client including design, typesetting and artwork.

## PMS
Refers to Pantone Matching System. A system for controlling accurate colour reproduction of printing inks. Pantone references are used universally. Each colour shade is given a number as in 'PMS 165 Red' Additionally there are a number of basic colours in the system which are given names as in 'Pantone warm red'

## Perfect binding
A bookbinding method in which pages are glued rather than sewn to the cover.

## PP
Printed pages as in '16 pp.' meaning a sixteen page brochure.

## Production

Work done to take a project from written form to the stage where it can be reproduced in the chosen media.

## Proofs

Proofing comes in various guises. Wet proofs from a printing press can be on the actual paper stock specified for the final run. Digital proofs give a very close rendering of the finished job and have the advantage that amendments can be made at this late stage without incurring the costs of new plates which would be required for new wet proofs. Designers digital print outs enable a check on all copy and content is correctly in place, but may not give and accurate rendering of the finished job. In this case it is always wise to see the actual job on the press to ensure quality is as expected. Newspapers will give a proof of the advertisement before publication, but not necessarily to the final printing standard.

## UV varnish

Used to highlight a specific part of the printed image with a gloss effect.

## Reversed out

Text appearing white on a black or coloured background as opposed to black or a colour printing on white.

## Rough / scamp / visual / concept

A quick hand drawn sketch of an idea. It can be for the layout of an advertisement, a brochure or even a logo.

## Run of paper (rop)

Advertising placed at the discretion of the publisher on pages alongside editorial content.

## Saddle stitched

A binding process in which a brochure or booklet is stapled through the middle fold of its sheets using saddle wire.

## Score

A pressed mark in a sheet of paper to make folding cleaner and easier.

## Self-cover

The paper used inside a booklet is the same as that used for the cover.

## Solus

An advertisement appearing on the page without any other advertiser. Note this does not necessarily mean that someone else's advertisement will not be placed on the opposite page.

## Stock

The paper, card or board used for printed items. Here you'll find a minefield of specifications, sizes, finishes and types of material. Apart from the publications in which your advertisement appears where you'll have no choice in the matter, paper comes in four basic finishes. Matt, a textured flat appearance; coated art, glossy and smudge-resistant when plain but tends to 'crack' when folded and marks easily if printed all over with colour; satin or silk, a similar feel to art but takes flat colour and folds better. However it does not reproduce photographs as brightly; cartridge which is best used for line work rather than photographs and full colour reproduction. Please note I've greatly over simplified the foregoing particularly when additional aspects of finish are considered. For example laid; embossed; hammered; linen and son on not to mention weights (see gsm). To select an appropriate paper for any job there is simply no alternative to handling examples and getting advice on the right selection. As far as sizes are concerned, forget the old foolscap and imperial measurements for the moment. These are very rarely used these days. The most common paper sizes now use the ISO standard comprising A, B, and C series. The system is designed so as each time a sub division is folded in half lengthways, the proportions of the original sheet are retained.Hence A4 folded in half equals A5, A5 folded equals A6 and so on through the entire series. The A series include the familiar A4 letterhead size and is seemingly also used for the majority of literature. The C series is for envelopes, C4 envelope being ideal for holding an A4 sheet, and C6 for A4 folded crossways. There is also the familiar DL envelope to take an A4 sheet folded longitudinally. The B series provides intermediate sizes for the A series but this is rarely used apart perhaps for B4 when a brochure needs to carry a bit more 'presence.' Of course you can use any size of printed item you choose. However, as most paper merchants supply ISO sized stock it is most cost effective to stay with ISO standards.

## Sheets
Generally used to define sizes of posters and billboards. A poster of 4 sheets is commonly used for outdoor advertising and most larger sizes are multiples of a four sheet. 6 sheet for pedestrian targeted street advertising increasing through 12, 16, 48 and 96 sheets for the large wide format advertisements.

## Typeface
The word most professionals use for 'font'.

## Voucher Copies
Copies of an advertisement taken from the media in which it appeared. These should be free of charge to a client as proof that the advertisement has appeared correctly.

# Useful contacts

### Advertising Standards Authority
Mid City Place
71 High Holborn
London WC1V 6QT
Telephone 020 7492 2222
www.asa.org.uk

### Advertising Association
7th Floor North
Artillery House
11-19 Artillery Row
London
SW1P 1RT
Telephone 020 7340 1100
www.adassoc.org.uk

### British Institute of Professional Photography
1 Prebendal Court,
Oxford Road,
Aylesbury,
Buckinghamshire, HP19 8EY.
Telephone 01296 718530
www.bipp.com

### Committee of Advertising Practice
Mid City Place
71 High Holborn
London WC1V 6QT
Telephone 020 7492 2222
www.cap.org.uk

## Chartered Society of Designers
1 Cedar Court
Royal Oak Yard
Bermondsey Street
London SE1 3GA
Telephone 0207 357 8088
www.csd.org.uk
CIPR

## Chartered Institute of Public Relations
32 St. James's Square
London SW1Y 4JR
Telephone 020 7766 3333
www.cipr.co.uk
Design Business Association
35 – 39 Old Street
London
EC1V 9HX
Telephone 020 7251 9229
www.dba.org.uk

## Design Council
34 Bow Street
London WC2E 7DL
United Kingdom
Telephone 020 7420 5200
www.designcouncil.org.uk

## The Institute of Practitioners in Advertising (IPA)
44 Belgrave Square
London
SW1X 8QS
Telephone: 020 7235 7020
www.ipa.co.uk

## MRS (The Market Research Society)

15 Northburgh Street
London EC1V 0JR
Telephone 020 7490 4911
www.mrs.org.uk

## Plain Language Commission

The Castle
29 Stoneheads
Whaley Bridge
High Peak
Derbyshire SK23 7BB
01663 733177
01663 735135
www.clearest.co.uk

# Index